Protecting Planet Earth

humanity, diversity and ecology

through Conscious Co-evolution

A manifesto for powerful change and a wake up call

to where the inner work and the outer work meet

Christopher Gladwell

Order this book at www.christophergladwell.com

Author: Christopher Gladwell
Editor: Christopher Gladwell
Cover Illustrator: Joshua Phoenix Harlow-Warnock

Note for librarians;
A cataloguing record for this book is available from
Bibliographic Data Services Limited (BDS)
Annandale House,
The Crichton, Bankend Road, Dumfries DG1 4TA

info@bibdsl.co.uk

Printed and bound by CPI Group (UK) Ltd, Croydon, CR0 4YY

ISBN: 978-0-9567922-8-0

Published by: www.christophergladwell.com

Protecting Planet Earth

humanity, diversity and ecology

through Conscious Co-evolution

A manifesto for powerful change and a wake up call to where the inner work and the outer work meet

Christopher Gladwell

What is the inner work?

The inner work is what we do to find out why we exist, who we are and what we're doing here.

This inner work gives us clarity, focus and insight beyond our personal stories, meanings and beliefs.

This work gives access to the wisdom that arises when we know from our intestines, our cells, our sinews and synapses that everything really is joined up, seamless and whole.

This inner work gives us a naturally arising compassionate understanding of how we humans struggle with fear, anxiety, rage, greed and all the suffering and diseases of separateness and the isolation and pain this creates.

This inner work gives us a naturally arising compassionate understanding of this illusion of separation, an illusion because everything is part of the seamless web.

This inner work gives us freedom from the myth of materialism, the illusion that having solid possessions gives us status or real security and that we are separate from the trees, the wind, the ocean, the planet or from each other.

This inner work gives us freedom from the myth of space-time, and reminds us that all that is has always been, is and always will be, beyond any bang, large or small, that was ever supposed to cause anything.

This inner work gives us purpose and passion to do what is necessary to facilitate the evolution of humanity, in a powerful and positive way.

The inner work gives us the energy to achieve our goals.

This inner work gives us knowledge of who we really are, our core-identity.

This inner work gives us freedom from fear and the courage to do what is right and true.

Without the inner work the outer work is unsustainable.

What is the outer work?

The outer work is the work of ecological and social sustainability and of empowered pro-social change.

We need a pro-social agenda that respects people and planet above profit and power-over or dominance.

Despite the delusions of the profit hungry and the power hungry, empirical science tells us conclusively that our planetary systems are changing in ways that do not serve the continuity of life on earth, and that we humans are responsible because of our continuing materialistic, consumption oriented culture.

It's still not too late to turn this monster of consumption and greed around, but it it is going to take concerted and mutually empowered action by all of us who want to create a sustainable planet for all our children and our children's children.

The outer work gives us a future.

The outer work gives us purpose, passion and possibility in creating sustainability, ecologically, socially and economically.

The outer work gives us the possibility of understanding our place in and as part of our eco-system, this planet.

The outer work needs the inner work as fuel, realised insight and the inspiration and stamina to know is needed and then to do it, together.

Where do the outer work and the inner work meet?

They meet in the human experience of the unified force of heart, mind and body.

They meet in the direct experience of being this earth, being the water, rain, rivers and ocean and being the air, the breath of plants.

They meet in the communities and choices we make to live a good life, in a wholesome way that frees us from the myth of separatist-materialism and its illusions.

They meet in the ways we change our world for the better, despite the obstacles of facing corporate, military, political and industrial might. These organisations are all run by people, people who have children and grandchildren, people who have hearts and minds, and people that do care, despite some of their behaviours supporting the machine of consumption and planetary desecration.

They meet in our personal practice and lives and how we live together as sometimes, messy human beings, managing our minds and feelings and hurting bodies with grace, compassion and care. They meet in the way we drop the strategies of the consumption culture, strategies of blaming, shaming and punishment. Instead we act from mutual responsibility, compassionate understanding, ecological intelligence and appropriate education.

They meet in the ways we laugh and can celebrate because of and despite the chaos of the separatist-materialist agenda and its ecocidal practices.

The meet in the ways we make love, dance and play together and the ways we work diligently and with purpose.

The inner and outer work meet in conscious co-evolution.

Conscious Co-evolution

My premise is that, throughout evolution, there is a consistent multi-faceted theme occurring, woven through space-time.
This loose theme is one of overall growth into greater, more expansive and more Self-reflective consciousness. As practitioners of conscious co-evolution we can acknowledge and work with this flow.
This section on conscious co-evolution is offering a dogma-free view, an exploration and an invitation to deepen in inquiry and community.

on Evolution

Evolution is really a process of co-evolution. Evolution is a function of inter-dependence and impermanence, nothing ever evolves alone.
People speak of the 'evolution' of a particular species such as bees or humans. Yet in reality nothing evolves alone. The concept of the selfish gene and survival of the fittest is a very single sided vision of evolution.
No organism is actually separate from its environmental milieu, a fish is also the ocean, it is 70% ocean plus 30% of the things it has eaten, all modified into a new temporary vortex of living organic matter and bio-energy.
A flowering plant can only evolve along with a pollinating insect. Both flower and insect are the process of interdependent co-evolution. All of life is the process of interdependent co-evolution. Organisms are not separate from their environment. The flow of water, minerals and atmospheric gases are also what that organism is.
Changes in the environment certainly influence an organism's survival, natural selection is accurate here. As environmental conditions change, and they do, then the genetic material that offers an advantage in those changed conditions will be selected for. Survival is not simply to the fittest individual though, it is to

the fittest community, the fittest gene-pool, the community with the best epigenetic expressions of their genes and to those whose changed behaviours are then supported by the successive genetic mutations that lifts them along the web of co-evolution.
We humans dramatically change our environment. We are already deeply engaged in unconscious, unaware co-evolution as we transform our world around us and affect the survival of countless of individuals and species around us.
We are now in the geological age called the Anthropocene. This is the name for the age where the main factor affecting ecological change is us, the human species. As we affect our environment we affect which genes are selected for.
We could, of course, make our environment so hostile that only cockroaches and Cyborgs could survive! We could also pay attention to the key-points of conscious co-evolution in this book and start to work towards stewardship of this planet instead of destruction and depredation.
What choice will you make?

What choice will we make together?

I consider the following key-points of conscious co-evolution worthy of attention, there will be other key-points equally worthy.
These key-points are intended to help us, as individuals, and as a species, pay attention to our place in the flow of co-evolution and how we consciously choose to work within this web.

When we work consciously with this flow, this seamless web, we are engaging in the vision of conscious co-evolution.
Aligned with conscious co-evolution, bringing mindful attention into all aspects of our daily life, we grow together in community that is conscious of the way we co-evolve.

Mindfulness is the attentive caring movement of the heart, it is compassion in action, what else could it really be? This mindfulness and compassion in action is the movement into conscious co-evolution.
The supreme state of compassion centred mindfulness is presence-being.
Some call the sentient quality of presence-being super-consciousness

and others pristine awareness. Either way, we are talking about our original nature, the nature of mind from which the content, imaginative process and creative explorations of mind arise.

Presence-being is a life-state in which one is heartfully (compassion centred mindfulness) aware of the ripples in space-time that are the consequence of every word, deed and action.

Buddha simply means 'awakened one' or 'switched on to the real'. Buddha Maitreya is said to be the future Buddha. Maitreya means 'friend of all'. The Maitreya principle is a metaphor for the time in human co-evolution when we all know, we all really get inseparability, that everything is part of the seamless web. With this recognition comes behaviour, we treat each other with simple love, respect, tolerance, human kindness and decency. We are all the body, mind, heart and soul of Maitreya, if you choose to work with that metaphor.
If not no problem, we are all part of the solution, in every moment and action of our lives.

Similarly, Vedic teaching clearly and consistently communicates that we are all Brahman, that everything is Brahman, and that Brahman is the totality, it is seamless flow, inseparability.
Brahman is the absolute and the relative flow, it is the many and the One, the One as the many and the many as the One. A German word for this is the Ubgrund.

Without trying to sell these teachings, that is not needed, these kind of teachings of seamlessness are rare in the western world of separate and materialist thinking, and as such offer a valuable counterpoint to the nihilistic futility promised by western life.

Native Americans talk of the Great Spirit, Wakan Tanka or Usen and again teach the inseparability and unity of all of life, we are all relations. When we get it, when we finally realise this, when we see and feel this, life is changed forever. When we live as the Ubgrund the only result is kindness to all, friendliness to all, respect to all, and love as and for all. We're a fair old way off this level of collectively evolved consciousness though.

The squabbling tribes of humanity are battling across the surface of this beautiful planet, this cosmic sanctuary for life, this amazing globe. What better way to describe our context other than cosmic sanctuary? With just the right mix of gases as an atmosphere, just the right temperature, just the right distance from our sun which is just the right size, with just the right amount of water and the right flow of warm earth heated at its core with earth mined by microbes to generate life like us. This blessed earth being destroyed by ignorance and stupid greed.

Conscious co-evolution seeks freedom from such ignorance. The very word ignore-ance tells is what it means. It is ignorant indifference. Ignorant indifference is not paying attention to what is true and real. It is failing to see the consequences of thoughts, words and deeds, failing to compute seamlessness.

Conscious co-evolution gives us some stepping stones.
All behaviour is to some degree context dependent. All ideas are informed by the time and place within which they are delivered. There are clear cultural contexts that inform methods of behaviour.

Methods of behaviour are simply ways to experientially, subjectively realise the seamless nature of reality, as totality, to touch with our hearts and thus to remember and know that we know absolutely nothing, and in knowing nothing be humbled and touched by everything.

Conscious co-evolution is where the inner work meets the outer work, at the edge of human evolution and eco-destruction.

This necessary outer work for our time is a vast web of transformations to make this beautiful planet socially and ecologically sustainable.

These transformations seen through the vision of conscious co-evolution include:-

- A new economy based on parity, need and sharing of resource rather than greed, profit motive and a vast inequality of wealth leaving bil lions in desperate poverty.

- Global systemic government rather than squabbling tribes in exclu sive territories and global ghettos.

- Transformation of child rearing and education systems from sec ond-rate cheap child care and schools focused on producing corpo rate lackeys to childcare being seen as the top priority and education being to build optimal brains and foster potential, globally.

- Preventative holotropic medical systems being prioritised and cura tive medicines being a supportive method of health care instead of a pharmaceutically loaded, symptom oriented, curative system.

- High value nutritionally dense food being optimally produced for the benefit of both environment and consumer, whilst highly processed nutritionally light belly filler is gradually eradicated from the human diet.

- Ecological intelligence and responsivity are made a paramount aspect of all global decision making and manufacturing processes.

- Gross national product is replaced with the happiness or wellbeing quotient.

- Decision makers and global stewards, from now on, are ecologically and emotionally intelligent as well as fiscally wise, compassionate and creative thinkers responding to pro-social needs with clear pro grammes to respond to those needs. These people would be involved in cybernetic management systems that are responsive to feedback loops and the flow of economic, social and environmental informa tion. This replaces profit motivated, psychopathological leaders who believe themselves to be independent of the environment and separate from their fellow humans. Such unhealthy leadership being a residue of our recently post-feudal history.

These are a few of the necessary transformation to make this planet socially and ecologically sustainable.
What kind of human being would facilitate and be content with such an ordered and responsive system?

It would need to be an individual who, as an adult, takes full responsibility for all of their thought processes, their emotional world and all of their behaviours.

It would be an individual who knows we are relational and that the 'social synapse' is also part of who we collectively are. Such an individual would know they are not an individual really, but a unique component of a social and ecological web of interdependence and dependent origination. This systemic realisation requires real ecological stewardship rooted in an embodied understanding of human and planetary interdependence.

Such a person would have taken responsibility for managing their central nervous system and be capable of deactivating their stress response and its behaviours at will. A powerful place to be.

Such a person would have developed their left pre-frontal cortex, anterior cingulate hub and capacity for the generation of gamma synergy brain wave state to the degree that they have developed the pro-social emotions of compassion, celebration of others success and resilient joy.

They would be aware and cognisant, capable of expressing and honouring the evolutionarily more ancient emotions such as hate, jealousy, anxiety, anger and depression arising from the enteric nervous system and amygdalic hub, whilst being able to feel, express, moderate and transform them into pro-social emotions.

They would be able to shift brain states to maintain physical, emotional and cognitive wellbeing, moving from beta, to alpha with ease. They would be able to access theta brain states during waking to facilitate rapid experience dependent neuro-plasticity, initiate creativity and evidence that rapid learning through their behaviours.

They may be able to access delta brain wave states with ease whilst remaining lucid in either dreams or waking consciousness. Lastly they would be able to access gamma spikes and gamma synergy to enhance creativity and to take their whole neurology into deep states of cohesive synergistic function and equanimity.

Children at school will be taught these skills along with how to sustain positive physical and electro-magnetic health through -

- Body based practices
- Breath based practices
- Practices of wellbeing psychology
- Optimal positivity
- Functional belief creation for positive health and creative outcomes
- Solution focused thinking
- Learning how to learn, self-directed learning
- Pattern recognition
- Problem solving
- Enhanced creativity
- Pro-social skills
- Relational reality of existence

...and other crucial learning experiences that are responsive to an unknown future need rather than how to satisfy the needs of a current job market that will be radically different in their lifetime.

Another essential skill is contentment. This is a result of an inner presence and satisfaction. Such presence does not use consumer goods as a means of esteem or finding wellbeing. Such presence does not chase security in material objects but knows security in itself and in its social connectivity.

What are these inner skills supporting and allowing such social, economic, ecological and political transformation?

Where are these skills coming from?

One of the key players in making sustainability sustainable and cultivating the possibility of an enhanced future where prosocial sustainability is known as equally important to ecological sustainability is the inner work.

The inner meditative work of conscious co-evolution is a technology for training the attentional circuits of the anterior cingulate cortex, the executive function of the left prefrontal cortex and generating gamma

synergic equanimity.
Such inner meditative work disinhibits the illusory force of the selfing systems of the posterior parietal and the insula and allows the deep embodied recognition of the seamless and ecologically interdependent nature of reality.

Conscious co-evolution is a systematic technology of wellness, physically, emotionally, cognitively, ecologically and in terms of our potential.

Conscious co-evolution is a crucial technology for the survival, wellbeing and continued co-evolution of the human species.
So what are the key-points of conscious co-evolution worthy of attention?

They are…

- Consciousness - self reflection and knowing one's deepest identity as pure awareness

- Complexity - of organisation and systemic relationships

- Core - our vertical bipedal relationship to gravity

- Communication - a co-evolutionary interpersonal art

- Conscious community - the only way we can survive as a species

- Creativity - the capacity to make tools, art, and new worlds

- Childcare - how we facilitate the development of future generations

- Compassion - the ability to deeply feel, to be touched and moved by another's existence and condition

- Cultivating pleasure - the desire to give and receive pleasure and know bliss

- Commitment and compersion - deep realtionship and the resolution of jealousy

- Currency - the methods and means of resource access and movement

- Carbon-silicon interface - the creation of informational technolo gy and artificial intelligence and how we as carbon based, DNA rich, neurologically complex bio-computers most effectively and skilfully interface with this

- Commensals and symbionts - the microbiome, the multitude of or ganisms that our life is bound up with and that we depend on

- Comedy - the aptitude to self reflect and generate humour out of the context in which we find our self

- Celebration and Ceremony - the ways we come together and craft shared meaning, generate deeper community and explore collective meaning making

- Conflict resolution - how we choose to utilise and transform the ener gies of conflict

- Contentment - the state of flow

- Conservation of diversity - maintenance of the web of life

- Collective decision making - how do we collectively decide on our course of action as a culture?

- Conscious culture creation - prosocial awareness of how we build culture

- Collective and concerted action - how to make positive change

If this evaluation of our co-evolutionary position is sufficiently accurate, then we could explore and follow this co-evolutionary path, by paying conscious attention, and working with clear intention and behaviour, in these key areas of co-evolutionary transition as a part of how to redirect our attention, imagination and behaviour towqards more pro-social outcomes than mere consumption.

I consider each of these key-points to be an art form, an art form that we could choose to explore and excel in, both as individuals, and as a collective.

Let's continue this journey of conscious co-evolution by asking...
How and why are we human beings currently the dominant species on this planet?

We clearly don't have big teeth, defensive armour, fur to keep us warm or vicious claws.
How did we even survive as a species?

Maybe we were directly 'created' by some divine power, maybe we are alien spirits inhabiting human form?

I don't believe this, despite the feeling I sometimes have of being very different from the humanity I see around me. No, I understand, appreciate and accept our fleshy lineage as co-evolutionary arising from prior mammals.
If, like me, you can look at your own nipples, your own body fur in the mirror and recognise that you are also an interesting species of bipedal vertical mammal, then great. If you're interested by the factors that led to us being the dominant life-form and where we might be heading, please enjoy what follows. Feel free to add to this narrative, this work and grow the vision of conscious and collective co-evolution.

As previously mentioned, co-evolution is influenced by the environmental demands on organisms. We influence and transform our environment through our behaviours. As we influence our environment we are unconsciously and unwittingly playing a hand in our own co-evolution. This matters for humans as there are so many of us, and we have a massive collective effect.

If we could look at what factors affect co-evolution; is there anything we could pay attention to that would facilitate our conscious and aware co-evolution, our survival and the wellbeing of our planet and it's myriad lifeform?

It is this inquiry that has led to these key-points.

I'm not seeking to offer the definitive view on this topic, I'm open to alternative views and better ways to understand the complexity of the context and time we find ourselves living in.

Consciousness

the first key to conscious co-evolution is self-reflective consciousness

Less complex creatures eat, respire, move, reproduce, expire, and that's about it. Such simple creatures have reflexive, innate instinctual responses to the world around them. Plants also have an array of reflexive responses to the world around them, whilst they too are sentient, indeed, at a micro level it is at times, difficult to make any clear distinction between plant sentience and animal sentience.
As lifeforms become more complex, their processing power, which includes a locus of identity, takes longer to grow and develop. Locus of identity is a functional development that allows for continuity of experience and ongoing relationships within a group. It is the locus of identity, or 'sense-of-self', that 'has' these experiences.
Remembered events (the past), apprehension about the future, narratives and meaning making all revolve around this sense-of-self, which is the 'one who acts'.

The 'I' feeling, the sense-of-self and it's self story are the self-construct. This self-construct becomes more robust, more complex and more involved in relationship as animals move into greater levels of socialisation. Now we have the self-construct as part of a group, it has its place, its stream of relating and all the stories and feelings associated with this. This is also what we are.
It's necessary for such a social creature to remember each relationship and relational dynamic. This memory allows effective engagement in future intra-group dynamics. We build narratives around what happened and what ours and others roles were. The important role of story or narrative in our experience as humans reflects this.

In many animal groups social interaction can be stressful and complex and lead to minimal reproductive success since it is mostly the alpha males and females who reproduce. In such groups there is a constant struggle for ranking, for being one of the alphas. Yet being in a group in any rank offers safety and identity. Outside of the group there is isolation, uncertainty and death. Early emotional drives function to keep us in the group.

As human life emerges, the self-construct is embedded within the family, the hunter-gatherer group. In such a group there is always the definition of the 'in-group' (us), and the 'out-group' (them). The in-group, the family, kin, group or tribe offers identity and safety. The out-group is different, alien, wrong, and not to be trusted.
All the reflexive patterns of being in the world including the self-construct and our cultural conditioning (being part of the in-group) are largely unconscious, out of the field of awareness. Any part of the neurological flow of information that bubbles up out of the unconscious into the global workspace, the arena of individuated consciousness, allows us the appearance of voluntary action. This global workspace is the seat of choice and, arguably, free will. We get to choose what to attend to or not within the spectrum of whatever is presented from unconscious process into conscious process. That appears to be the only choice available to us.

As the social human evolved through agrarian and industrial societies into the contemporary technological world, the possibilities of emergent-consciousness changed. Gradually, we could separate our self-construct from total identification with the qualities of the group, qualities such as social organisation, orthodox religion and group identity. Once achieved, we now have the possibilities of identifying with a level of awareness where we can recognise each of us as being mutual and equal residents, inter-relational residents of this planet. In other words, we are all in this together and we know it.

The movement from close proximity to wild nature, through industrialised culture, has led to a disassociation from any deep ecological level of consciousness. We have not lost our place as part of nature, though most of us are now utterly unconscious of this place, or worse, in denial of this reality from which we cannot escape. This feeling and awareness of ecological intimacy is in the process of being reclaimed through re-wilding, and is being more deeply understood by many of us. This reclaimed ecological intimacy in conjunction with the new possibilities of trans-global consciousness, which are increasingly available to us all,

courtesy, partly of the internet and contemporary culture, gives great possibilities of a powerful new culture. This new culture could be one in which we evolving humans will steward this planet effectively.
The complexity, the fly in the ointment, is the vested interests of those that feel 'in possession' of land and resources, those who control production and drive consumption for their own ends. Those that feel powerful and in control will not easily want to let go of their feelings of power, even though that pathological power is what's destroying our planet. These interests also have to change to honour the reality of the situation we are in.
Who will help them?

How will we help liberate these beings from their entrenched and limited views?

Real power is mutual. Dominance and its necessary sibling, submission is the way of archaic feudalism.
Mutual empowerment, responsibility and collective responsivity is the way of the future.

This is by no means an authoritative outline of emergent consciousness. Emergent consciousness arises through the co-evolution of life-form and is dependent on co-evolution. Conscious co-evolution recognises this process and works with cultivating this systemic, deep-ecological awareness along with trans-global consciousness.
Insight arising through awareness of conscious co-evolution, teaches us that the whole universe can be helpfully seen as a play of sentience. This doesn't have to be the empirical truth, I'm uninterested in dogma creation, I'm interested in liberation and crafting a pro-social, ecologically intelligent future.

As we deepen in meditative awareness, the inner work, we subjectively experience this flow of co-evolution, systemic and integral connection, inter-dependence and vast awareness. We don't need to make this subjective experience a dogma, yet it is liberating to feel the continuity of consciousness as if the vibrating waves and particles of energy and matter that we also are, were all rippling with consciousness, all the field of subtle awareness.
Initially, in our subjective experience it feels like there is sentience

(consciousness/awareness) and then there is the movement of impermanent flowing things. These two sides to reality are often mentioned in yogic philosophies as consciousness and matter, principle and process, or emptiness and form. This level of awareness is a fundamental realisation that places the emergence of individuated consciousness, as the self-construct, within the matrix of nature or form.

As we deepen in witness consciousness, these appearances of two things gets exaggerated, until the witness itself dissolves. Then we experience emergent consciousness as a function of the cosmos that is to our eyes of contemplation none other than scintillating sentience. This is the role of meditation.

This next level of realisation that occurs is that this play of the two, sentience and impermanence, unicity and multiplicity, witness and witnessed, subject and object is all a grand illusion. The two are one inseparable matrix. Sentience, space and all movements of things as space are one beautiful exquisite dance. This is what yogis have often called non-dual realisation.

So we have the co-evolution of individuated consciousness, which itself allows systemic or deep ecological realisation. This level of co-evolution also allows trans-global consciousness and finally opens as cosmic consciousness.

The subjective experience of cosmic consciousness, or vast awareness, for want of better expressions, transcends and includes systemic and trans-global awareness.

All movement blissfully and intimately embraces all that is deeply still. Sentience and space are known, sensed and felt as ecstatic lovers, perpetually in orgasmic blissful embrace. One sees this kind of imagery in Tantric iconography. The subjective experience of meditators is that the heart of the cosmos is love, bliss, awareness and presence-being.

Conscious co-evolution is systemic, it places us as impermanent organisms in a healthy relationship with our eco-system.

Conscious co-evolution is trans-global, it places us in mutual and cooperative relationships with all members of humanity and co-creates the unfolding of a new global civilisation.

Conscious co-evolution is cosmic and ultimately realises the nature of reality as sentient space and spacious sentience, the two as one, the one as two.

Conscious and aware co-evolution requires self-reflective process and knowing ones deepest identity as this awareness, as the pristine awareness that predates, pervades and is the cosmos.

I propose that a 'civilisation' that encourages attention and action towards conscious co-evolution, a civilisation that encourages and promotes systemic, global and cosmic consciousness, would be an advanced and civilised civilisation.
How will we co-create such a civilisation?

Where do we begin?

So, lets do this inner work and switch on the level's of development we are capable of and make the outer work work.

Complexity

this second key to conscious co-evolution is complexity

When we look at the stream of co-evolution we can see an increase in biological complexity from palaeohistory to the present day. From single celled organisms evolution has flowed to create the more complex and more recent mammals such as us.
Our biological complexity is such that, unlike our ancestral amphibians, we can no longer regenerate body parts very well. Amphibians can re-grow limbs and some reptiles can re-grow tails, even though they are nowhere near as good as the originals, their new tails still function. We can re-grow skin, muscle and bone if it is damaged. We also constantly grow new neural synapses and neural sheaths with new use. These neural changes are related to our experiences in the world, which is the root of neuroplasticity. With our cognitive and creative capacities we are learning to grow new synthetic body parts and these are being successfully used in modern medicine. As well as our biological complexity we have a high level of social complexity.

Increasing social complexity is also a theme of human history. From hunter-gatherers through to agrarian villages, from barbaric feudal autocracies through to our (hopefully) more tolerant democracies, there is a general trend towards increasing complexity of social organisation. Understanding this flow of emergent complexity, we can choose through Engaged Yoga practices to consciously work with both aspects of biological and social complexity. The transformation of decision making structures from autocratic dominance to mutually self-managing communities could be seen to evidence this co-evolutionary flow. Competition is a dynamic where one individual or group of participants wins a particular outcome. Cooperation and collaboration in balance with appropriate competition or 'coopetition', as it is usefully understood, is a way this emerging complexity can be effectively worked with, as a win-win-win scenario.

Generating global understanding of the common ground between us all invites more cooperation, collaboration and coopetition. We are all in it together, we all need air, clean water, good food, shelter and human connection. Recognising this common ground could encourage us to enable all citizens of this planet to contribute to our collective wellbeing with their full potential.

Having members of our species unable to meet their potential and unable to share their gifts is a ridiculous waste of human resource.
When material resources are concentrated into the hands of the elite 'few', resources are then unavailable to provide for the necessary support and education of the 'many'.
Is greed and competition really a particularly sensible or sustainable way to govern a planet when it wastes so much human resource?

The thing about dis-eases, whether they are individual or epidemic, medical or social, is that they have to be diagnosed before the appropriate dose of medicine can be administered.
From the view of conscious co-evolution, humanity is suffering from a bad case of separate-materialism with its symptoms of fear, greed, envy, jealousy, nihilism, depression and hatred.

When we humans finally realise we are not separate, that indivisibility is how things really are, then cooperation, collaboration and friendly coopetition becomes the modus operandi, rather than seen as some wacky 'off the wall' behaviour. When we humans finally realise that separate lumps of stuff floating in space-time, is not how things really are, then cooperation, collaboration, sharing and friendly coopetition becomes the modus operandi.

When we humans finally realise we are not separate from the planet or the rest of life, that indivisibility is really how things are, then the governance of the planet would not be left to vested interest groups, party political agendas, or corporations operating from the model of separate materialism. Leaders with questionable understandings of how things really are would not be tolerated. Leaders who know and behave as if everything were inseparable, indivisible and a vast seamless unicity as diversity would be the norm.

When we humans finally realise we are not separate, that indivisibility is how things really are, then seeking common ground and cultivating real civilisation rooted in greater consensus, communication, compassion and transparent clarity of decision-making will be the norm.

So, the second key to conscious co-evolution is paying attention to complexity and creating co-evolutionary civilisation. The inherent demands of this are for cooperation, collaboration, coopetition, communication and understanding the common ground.
Each individual, encouraged and able to contribute and share their gifts effectively, along with a culture of consensus and transparent clarity in decision-making would be the norm.
This could well be the way forward, what are your thoughts?

What is stopping us?

I say, let's bring it on, let's consciously co-evolve and co-create a civilisation rooted in cooperation, collaboration, coopetition, communication and understanding the common ground.

Our Core

the third key is uniquely human, the vertical core line

With their flat feet, long iliac pelvic bones, and lumbar spine that cannot extend sufficiently to allow vertical bipedal movement even the apes cannot walk upright, vertical in their core like we do.

Vertical bipedal movement means that when we walk we are imbalanced 80% of the time. Our body is loaded on just two points of contact, the feet, and the vertical compression through our system presents different challenges to those experienced by our quadrupedal mammalian cousins.

One of these challenges in contemporary living is the collapse of the 'front line' of our body. With no skeletal structure between the ribs and pelvis the front line of our body easily collapses under the influence of weak muscles and gravity. Weak muscles of lift, arise from our lack of floor sitting, squatting and coming to standing from these positions.

This front line collapse also squashes the organs in the abdomen, reduces breath efficiency through impinging on the diaphragm and reduces the natural dynamic lift of the pelvic floor. A chronic version of this collapse might also include pronation or collapsed medial arches of the feet in standing. It will also include medially rotated femurs, lordotic lumbar spine, medially rotated shoulder blades and anteriorly rotated shoulders. This position along with a head shifted forward, suspended from the upper trapezius and spinal erector muscles means these muscles can no longer be effectively used to move the head.
But then who needs to?

Who needs to move when food comes directly to our door and the screens that fill our lives flood us with entertainment?

This sort of collapse is epidemic and a recipe for debilitating physiological, skeletal, and muscular problems. This collapse into forward flexion in the body, which is also the physical response to fear and stress, reduces breath efficiency and cannot sustain physical or psychological

wellbeing.
Like the egg and chicken question, does physiology precede attitude or attitude precede physiology?

The solution to front line collapse and its physiological, structural and psychological complications is Yoga of the Living Body and related body and mind based practices.
The solution is to engage in regular practices that enable the familiarisation and balance of the forces of gravity in the body throughout our structure whilst also cultivating embodied awareness.
Helpful practices that facilitate the flexible and elastic tissues of the myofascia to remain elastic and encourage optimal function include fascially intelligent yoga, pilates, martial arts, alexander technique, feldenkrais, fascial fitness and so on.
Central nervous system (CNS) management like we find in practices of conscious co-evolution is allied to these practices of optimal function. The alliance is deeper embodied awareness of all our function and the enhancement of optimal function in all areas of our existence.
These techniques, balanced with practices for clarifying the ancient enteric nervous system and it's relationship to our more recent neurological structures all lead to a quality of life that makes sense of our increased potential for longevity.
Would you prefer a long life with reduced quality of life, or with optimal function and a higher quality of life?

Practices that complement this neuro-somatic work are meditation, mindfulness and relaxation skills. The increasing levels of empirical support for these practices points to their contemporary value.

Fascially oriented movement practices are being proven to support the human bipedal form into older age, leading to positive health and wellbeing. Fascially destructive forms of movement practice such as aggressive yoga, styles of movement that shorten muscles and compress the skeleton and create damaging forces through the joints due to poor function, all lead to illbeing.

Meditation has been linked to positive epigenetic effects, stress release and regrowth of telomeres. Telomeres are the caps on our genetic component, our chromosomes. Telomeres when reduced initiate cell

death. Enough cell death equates to organ death and the death of us as an organism. This increase in the size of telomeres through meditative practice is related to increased longevity. With increased longevity we need increased quality of life, which grows through mindful living, altruistic behaviour and finding value and purpose in life. Meditation also invites greaqter vaule and purpose in life.
Meditation can also positively change the way brains work leading to greater relational wellbeing. This means we have better communities and enjoy our human interactions more. Mindful living is the requisite step in our human development that really honours this profound leap from four legs to two and all that goes with this.

So, when you walk be aware of the miraculous process of placing one foot in front of the other. When you talk be aware of the role of vertical standing. Vertival standing led to us facing each other with our vulnerable ventral surfaces.This vulnerability leads to the need for socialising, which leads to the need for advanced communication and the cerebral cortex that goes with this.

Our vulnerable ventral surfaces facing each other tend to be compensated for with emotional armour and all manner of other defences. Just go to a city and see the range of defensive means, from newspapers to mobile phones, all used to divide us off from our scary and unknown neighbours.

As you use your hands, maybe to hold that phone, be aware that vertical bipedal movement was what freed up our hands. Hands freed from being two of the four feet allowed for the use of tools. Hands and the brain that go with them, have crafted everything in our world that we so easily take for granted.

Hands allow us to touch, to eat, and to share as we do. So much is taken for granted. Instead of taking anything for granted, let's step, or even dance into the light of conscious co-evolution through working effectively with and from our core.

Wherever we go with our conscious co-evolution, the core and working from the core has a key role to play.

Communication

the fourth key is the art of communication

The art of communication is an evolutionary art and an evolutionary act. It is evolutionary because when used effectively it draws us into closer bonding, greater cohesion and greater collective power.

The art of communication (as opposed to misinformation, orwellian speak, persuasion engineering or alternative truthing) is revolutionary because it will not accept or tolerate what was, just because it was, seek to trick you, manipulate you or sell you things you don't need.

Communication requires deconstruction of what was, as well as construction of what will be.

Communication requires understanding and compassionate listening as well as clarity of expression.

Communication requires us to separate our observations, our judgements and opinions, our feelings and our requests for things to be different from each other. Real communication requires such compassionate clarity.

Our cerebral cortex is capable of deciphering a complexity of sounds, facial expressions and gestures through both our visual and auditory senses. We have an amazing set of vocal cords with which to make an array of sounds and can communicate complex meanings with ease. All of these functions in synergy are all reasons why we are currently the dominant species on this planet. The way we are behaving, this is unlikely to last.

To flow consciously and positively with our co-evolutionary circumstance, we would do well to enhance and develop the art of communication.
We are always in communication, even if we say nothing we're still

communicating. The question is -
What do we want to be communicating?
And, can we communicate more effectively and with greater skill?

Much human communication still includes...

- Uninvolved listening where people are planning their response
- Culturally conditioned taboos
- Culturally conditioned and collusive dialogue
- Reflexive responses
- Focused on supporting our neurotic, obsessive, egocen tric, ethnocentric and religiocentric viewpoints

To cultivate the art of communication, the following seventeen facets of this jewel, the art of communication prove useful. Of course there may well be more…

1. Interoception - the capacity to sense deeply into our own biological system and listen to its needs and desires.

2. Emotional literacy and intelligence - the capacity to know our own feelings and be able to effectively and clearly communicate them separate from our judgements and requests to others to behave differently.

3. Sit with feelings - To be able to sit with our feelings and not respond to them reflexively. We will then not be making addictive demands on others based on the flow of feelings moving through us. We can also then separate the feeling from any need we have so that our communication with each other is less emotionally charged, less reflexive and operating from greater clarity. We can talk about our feeling states, our needs and our viewpoints as separate but related aspects of our inner flow.

4. Heart based (compassionate) listening - the capacity to deeply listen to all the parts of oneself and others from a place of unconditional positive regard. Unconditional positive regard means we don't judge the essence of another person though whether or not we appreciate their behaviours.

5. Empathy of understanding - understanding that we're all learning to love, all learning to live in love. Understanding that we all make mistakes and that this is a large part of our learning process.

6. Desire to learn - consciously understanding and being playful with our non-verbal communication, our body language and pheromonal communication. We are then more willing to explore, play and learn in the theatre of human behaviour, and perhaps less likely to take it all personally and close down in fear or withdrawal.

7. Knowing our deepest identity - when we know who we are as our original nature, as pristine awareness, we wont be grasping at anything to feel safe. In this way toxic fear and her many children are slowly eliminated from communication. What remains is clear awareness and it's feeling state of love.

8. Knowing we are all in this together - we consistently seek the common ground.

9. Give up the blame game - we understand the complexities of flow so that we no longer seek to apportion responsibility for arising problems in other people's 'back yards', nor in our own. Our primary focus is now positive and solution focused. We understand the complex weave of how things arise and we now seek to create an empowered future from whatever is arising.

10. Willingness to suspend our own 'viewpoints' for the greater collective good - this capacity and willingness is balanced with an understanding that our viewpoints, if clearly expressed, may well serve the collective good. This is the art of consensus.

11. An abiding interest in conflict resolution - rather than conflict creation, continuity of conflict, or conflict management. Who does conflict serve? The art of resolution and mediation is a facet of the art of communication.

12. Wise discrimination - the art and practise of value, knowing what is truly important. What is wise? How do you know? How do we know?

13. Drop unskilful comparison, it eliminates joy.

14. Heal shame, it's utterly toxic.

15. End the complaining. There is a theory that an evolutionary aspect of human brains is to find the negative, what is wrong, what went wrong and who is responsible. Many humans, even though they have wealth, food, shelter, clean drinking water, computer technology and more, still complain. We can entrain our brains to find and express positivity. It's not that difficult to do.

16. Sustain a good sense of humour - sense of humour deficit is often a sign that we are starting to take it all a bit personally! We also recognise that one persons sense of humour is not another's.

17. Is it kind? Is it necessary? Is it true? If you answer yes to all three then communicate. If not, be quiet, it only causes suffering.

This fourth key to conscious and aware co-evolution is the art of communication.
Let's develop communication on every level, including all the subtleties described above manifesting through our non-verbal and physical to emotional, cognitive and ecological behaviours.
Remember communication is behaviour, knowing is doing.

Enhanced communication is a key part of our ongoing co-evolution.

Conscious Community

the fifth key to conscious and aware co-evolution is the art of community

Conscious Co-evolution is always workable. Workable means we can see it, touch it, feel it and work with it, there's movement and we can see what we are doing to create difficulties and problems or solutions with our minds.

Every moment is an opportunity to know and rest in our original nature of simple goodness. That's right, goodness. Unlike the view of original sin from our western religious inheritance, the yogic view is that the pure awareness that is the base nature of mind is pure compassion, pure goodness and that this goodness is distorted into unkindness and fear through cultural conditioning. Even if original goodness is a misunderstanding, (can thousands of meditators be wrong?) original sin is an unhelpful teaching.

When we understand and train our brains through the inner work of meditation we can see how we complicate things, generate dissatisfaction, unnecessary complexity, warfare and suffering.
We can see how we generate tapestries of narrative and meta-narrative, weaving sensation, feeling and ideas into stories of complexity, dissatisfaction, moral supremacy and so on.
We can see how we craft viewpoints that need defending or from which to attack others, and we can choose to do something differently with our viewpoint creation skills, we can choose to become an artist of belief rather than a soldier of belief.

These keys of conscious co-evolution are potentially a method to begin to feel and see the issues we face and invite the individual and collective steps that may help us co-evolve powerfully. These steps are not prescriptive, they're invitations to inquiry and insight. Flowing as awareness and with awareness in conscious co-evolution, allows us to thrive in the changing conditions we face and will continue to face.

The collective alternative, given our capacity to dominate and destroy each other and our environment, is extinction. Let's be blunt, extinction means the death of us, our friends and loved ones and our children and our children's children. Extinction doesn't just happen to other species and other people!

It's probably important to understand that no matter what we do, we are never not in community. Let me say that again as it's so important to understand, no matter what we do, we are never not in community. Even people sitting in caves are in community, the breath they breathe is also our breath.
Community is all of us, everyone, including those we know and love, those we live amongst and those we share this planet with, we really are all neighbours, all relatives.

Community in this sense is the concentric circles of the interdependent web of connection. Community is the place of communion, the spatial and temporal centre for shared existence. Without community there is no humanity.
We are a relational species. We do not exist without community.
We are a species within an ecolgical web, without other species we do not exist, and cannot exist. There is a limit to how much species extinction the web of life can take before it too collpases into another mass extinction.

The art of community is growing beyond unconscious conditioned community and into conscious community.

To understand conscious community it's useful for us to have some direct experience of the deepest truth of our subjective existence.
This 'truth' as vibrant livingness is simply that we are, in essence, pure awareness.
Pure awareness has a feeling sense to it of compassion, goodness or even love. In other words the feeling of awareness or consciousness in its most original form is love. We are all this. This is what people experience when they go deep into the inner work.

We also have common ground, we all breathe, we all share beating hearts and all have centres of gravity and feel our feet or some part of

our bodies on the ground. We all need food, water, shelter and love. When we know our bodies as flowing earth, water and air.
When we see that the heat of our muscles came from sunlight through food and that we are all the same, we start to get a sense of unicity. When we see the ways that we are formed through emotional relationship, and how our ideas and concepts and beliefs are all built out of relationship, we can stop seeing ourselves as independent.

Independence is an illusion, we are all inter-dependent. When we see that we're all built of relationship, we can begin to honour community and grow conscious community.

Older traditions have called the direct experience of unicity Brahman, Buddha, Shiva, God, Goddess, Sat-chid-ananda, Wakan Tanka, Original Nature and more recently the Ubgrund.
This truth of each one of us as beginninglessly enlightened non-dual essence, continuously co-evolving as awakening, learning, vibrant process is that we're all participants, inter-relational participants, in community.

Community is a method of conscious co-evolution. The pro-social method of conscious community creation recognises that each of us has the potential to support each others mutual arising. We support our 'relatives' in living as this direct experience of scintillating truth in relationship to each other.

Conscious community then moves from being a method to become the vehicle and the living expression of conscious co-evolution.
We become a community of Buddhas and Buddhas to Be or whatever other expression you prefer to describe our greatest and limitlessly creative, actualised and compassionate potential.
What does such a community offer?

Such a community offers sanctuary, support, challenge, communion and celebration.

Sanctuary is a place where we can rest in the experience of love, presence and awakened community.

Challenges, as appropriate and necessary, from our loving celebrants in community, help us to remain in presence, awareness and responsibility.

Support helps us face our challenges and issues, whilst deepening in practices of yogic method, insight and realisation.

Communion is the sharing of love, realisation and deep joy.

Celebration is the coming together in joy, appreciation and gratitude of the members of the community and collectively sharing and expressing this dance of inter-dependent appreciation.
How do we grow such community?

Honesty, integrity, presence, awareness and willingness to both communicate and take responsibility for all of our thoughts, feelings and behaviours, allows the development of conscious co-evolutionary community.

We each take individual responsibility for all of 'our' thoughts, feelings and behaviours, and the consequence and impact of these in the world. No one else is to blame, no one makes us think, or feel, or do anything.

As community members we assume total responsibility for resolving 'our' conditioning and yet rest in the openness and sustenance of the community of realisers.
To sustain such openness we cultivate integrity, profound awareness and willingness to face the truth of what is, with resolute inquiry and ruthless compassion.
Conscious community then becomes the community of the realisers.
We make manifest, we make real, conscious co-evolution.
Who is your conscious community?

When, how and with whom will you co-create, through your commitment and involvement, conscious community in a sustainable and integral way?

As conscious community we recognise we're all in this together, we're all family, all relatives. We play, work and share together to help each other discover our unique way of moving deeper into the vision and realisation of 'Truth'.

Members in community seek common ground, clear communication, resolution, responsibility, greater love, deeper wisdom, more joy, more peace and communal stewardship and sharing of this earth and it's resources.

Conscious community is a mirror reflecting back our strengths, weaknesses and blind spots, if we are prepared to see them. We see and know who we are, reflected in the hearts and minds of every member of our community.

Members support each other as they reveal and resolve shadow. Members take responsibility for their psycho-emotional states and for the wellbeing of the community.

Conscious community offers and invites a sustainable way into our own hearts and minds.
Living more and more fully in the heart of our being, we find mutual support in each other's struggles and successes, in each other's development and simple pleasures. Members celebrate each other's joy and success.

Members share commitment to each other's growth and development in conjunction with a commitment to the well-being and mutual growth of socially and ecologically sustainable community.

Members share love and learn to live in love. Love is simply the feelings of consciousness.

Conscious community offers the possibility of co-creating culture and a mutually empowered future.

Conscious community is realised inter-dependence in action.
Are you ready for the path of loving responsibility and sustainable community?

Let's practice the art of sustainable conscious community.

What's stopping us?

The fifth key of conscious co-evolution is the art of conscious community, which allows us to work together even more effectively and in harmony.

When we recognise all the myriad species of our planet as our 'community' as if we were all related, aren't we? Then our communities will include these myriad species and give living room to them as well.

Creativity

I would like us to pass on a habitable and beautiful planet to all our children and our children's children.
Why would we pass on a desecrated, polluted, war torn and embattled planet when we are capable of so much more?

the sixth key is enhanced creativity

We are the first mammal with fully opposable fingers and thumbs. This allows us to manipulate objects and make tools. Of course this capacity is connected to a cerebrum that can take creative perspectives.
Creative perspectives allow us to take a step back, up, or aside in our mind, and view any object or process from a new, different or abstract angle. It is this capacity to abstract our viewpoint and temporarily dissociate from an object, process or person and find a new place of perspective, ot seeing.
It's this new perspective connected to our desires and interests of course, that allows us to fashion tools and make art.
We are the tool making and art-making mammal.
No other creature makes art in quite this way. All other creatures that appear to be creative, such as bower-birds are driven by simple innate drives. Lets explore our unique creative potential a little more.

This capacity to abstract our viewpoint and temporarily dissociate from an object, process or person can also be subverted by conditioned egoic drives into destructiveness.
The shadow side of our artistic capacities is our ability to take life very personally, feel offended or upset by arising phenomenal events and operate from this place of dissociation.
From this separated viewpoint, with all its associated agenda, we create new methods of destruction, torture and degradation for anyone we perceive as different, as the object to our superior subjective viewpoint.
Different can mean different tribe, different nation, different religion, different family, different ideas, different belief or different anything in fact.
We can make egoic self-story positions and 'others' out of any perceived

difference.
We can also make art out of any perceived difference. The choice is ours!
So, what is creativity?

Creativity is, perhaps, “an inspired response to phenomena from the experience of being human”, as my friend Loren put it. It’s certainly arising out of a basic interest in phenomena. We have to be interested in something and cultivate an affinity with it to begin to manipulate and see its potential. We also have to assume two positions...

• The first is the place of involved abstraction so we can move the object around in our mind-scape.

• The second is the combined willingness, desire and ability to thoroughly engage with the material we are investigating. We have to be willing to explore and play.

This is as true of sculpture, music and painting as it is of creative technology and creative environmental and social systems.

Art is a flow of interest and engagement. Our life is our art in this sense, and the ‘canvas’ is our mind-scape, our feeling-scape, our body, our relationships and our environment.
How will you choose to craft your art of love and scintillating wisdom out of, and through life?

Maybe life is art, period.
Sadly, many of us don’t get it and keep painting everything in our world grey or magnolia! Many of us build sculptural testimonies to life wrapped in barbed wire and ecocidal nuclear missiles, uber penile towers pointing to the sky and lanscapes smothered in plastic waste and so on.

‘Life sculpting’ is what we can choose to do when we begin to recognise the spacious freedom between stimulus and response.

It’s the meditative space of presence, felt it in the mind, heart and body that we can move from, dance with and sculpt our lives and our world from, let's do this.

The sixth key is enhanced creativity. Let's explode our creativity and co-create a fabulous, ethical, compassionate and sustainable world built from the visioning of the space of deep presence.

Childcare and Education

the seventh key to conscious co-evolution is childcare and education

The most important task for our species and culture is providing for and raising the next generation. All other activity and business support this one aim.
One might think this wasn't the case given the low levels of funding and resource allocated to childcare, and the minimal priorities given to this crucial evolutionary role.

Child mortality in Victorian times in the poorer communiites in the U.K. was over fifty percent. Even amongst wealthy elites it was over ten percent. Nowadays in the U.K. the infant mortality rate is well under one half of one percent, that is a powerful change in under two hundred years.
Experiences in the womb and during birthing affect the development of every child. The level of love a mother feels in her world, for herself and for her unborn child also affect these crucial early phases of development and the prenatal learning a baby experiences.

We know that the hypo-thalamic-pituitary axis (the HPAA), is set up in the first six months of life. This HPAA is the core line of endocrine glands along the midline of the body that determines our basic chemical response to life circumstances. These glands release metabolic hormones, stress hormones, and sexual hormones. Authentic yoga seeks to bring balance to these glands.
When a baby is held, loved, nourished, cared for and is helped with its emotional management then these glands then set at an optimal level. If the foetus and infant experience un-love, stress and fear then these glands are set up to manage a world of fear and un-love.

Babies cannot self-regulate, they cannot calm and comfort themselves. This comfort and emotional regulation needs to be offered to them by loving adults.

Old school behaviours of letting children cry themselves to sleep simply riddle the developing brain with toxic quantities of stress hormones whilst setting the HPAA up for a life of relative anxiety, uncertainty and the feelings of separation and other mental health problems.

Being riddled with stress hormones at an early age predisposes the brain for poor internal communication. The part that feels and the part that can express feelings will be unable to communicate effectively. Dysfunctional unloving parenting exposes the baby to a risk of emotional illiteracy and problematic relationships, probably like its parents. Brains riddled with stress hormones at an early age are prewired with parts of the brain that are lacking in pleasure receptors, they cannot feel pleasure in the same way as others who have these pleasure receptors. Brains riddled with stress hormones at an early age are also set up for ineffective concentration.

Brains grown in toxic, stress rich environments act as if they are faced with constant threat and at risk of danger. Such brains are always on hyper-alert for the next threat. This is no way to live life fully.

Babies are 'tribal animals', they need to be near their significant loving elders (parents, grandparents, siblings, etc), to be seen, and to develop optimal emotional and mental function.

Being seen and responded to helps the infant build its neuro-synapses. The baby brain is building its neurological network for at least the first five years of life. Having its preverbal communications and emotional world fully responded to in consistently loving ways is crucial for optimal human functioning.

Loving attentive significant elders are the ones who can understand these communications. Leaving an infant with other elders who might not understand its early communication attempts so well is a recipe for that infant to shut down those aspects of its brain.

Love does matter.

Having come from a warm, dark, pulsing and living womb the transition into brightness, edges and touch is demanding enough without the isolation some babies get. This isolation occurs when the child is put in cots or cribs and left to cry itself to sleep. Babies love to be held close, touched and comforted for at least the first six months. In my family world babies are kept close to or on their significant elders for the first six months. Having an earthing celebration where the child is formally laid on the earth in a circle of family and friends is a way to give the child its second birth, from the womb to the warm flesh of the family, and from the family onto the living earth.

Breastfeeding gives babies liquid love, builds immunity and healthy brains and develops a continued bonding with mother. Mother's milk offers appropriate nutrition and also emotional comfort and is to be encouraged as much as possible. Some women are choosing not to breastfeed so as to not change the shape of their breasts. Some women are choosing to have caesarians instead of vaginal births so as to not change the shape of their vaginal orifice. Vaginal birth fires up bonding neuro-chemicals such as oxytocin and a raft of endorphins that give the next level of bonding after gestation as well as immune function from the microbial coating given through natural birth.
Obstetric violence in some countries is preventing women from expressing the freedom of choice in how to birth and how to bond with their offspring.
Authentic and appropriate somatic, breath, meditation, visualisation and relaxation practices build bonding between mother and the infant inside the womb. They also strengthen and open the mother's body ready for a healthy and optimal, even ecstatic birth.
Yes! It is not just okay to feel ecstatic and even orgasmic during birthing and breastfeeding, it's normal.

I question the psychological development of any man who cannot love a woman whose body has changed after giving birth to his child. If he is so addicted to a particular form that he cannot support the mother of his child as she goes through her profound physical changes and rebuilds her body, what shape is his heart and mind in.
Where is the love?

Breasts are primarily mammary glands and offer so much nourishment on every level to a newborn child that it is, (unless there are some medical complications that prevent this) in my opinion close to abusive or neglectful to wilfully withhold that magical nourishment and contact from a newborn child.
The milk bliss a baby feels after breastfeeding as it curls against its mother's body cannot be matched with bottles of formula.
The composition of breast milk changes through the day with the

evening milk containing components that encourage sleep.
There is also evidence that shows that babies regulate their breath through resonance with mother's breath, as long as the mother is not desensitised with alcohol, tobacco or other narcotics. Cot deaths may be more likely for women who isolate their children in cots and cribs.

The ideal scenario for a healthy baby is as natural a birth as possible to a relaxed happy mum who cares for her child with as much touch, holding and breastfeeding as that child needs. An enlightened culture would support this process for every mother.
A barbaric, primitive and uncivilised culture would simply put profit and economic power before the wellbeing of mother and child.

The mother's ante-natal preparation and parent's pre-conception preparation would ideally include a few years of somatic practice and meditation. For the father, this will help to prepare him to support both mother and children. For the mother somatic practice will help her body be as open and strong as possible for birthing. Breath training will assist the birth process. Deep relaxation, meditation and vibrational work such as mantra can help prepare for the arduous period of sleeplessness and demands that characterise the early stages of the mother and baby relationship.
As a father, I chanted to my children as they rested in their mother's womb, when they came out into the world they knew my voice already. When I sing to them or hold them I am a familiar part of their world, and they can relax even more in my arms. As a man, the most amazing and beautiful thing I have ever seen and partaken in is the mother of my children giving birth, watching the babies head emerge and then the profound vision of beauty of the mother and baby as the little infant feeds from the breast.
If we really are to co-create an enlightened society then we need to prioritise attention to care and preparation for mothers and fathers to be, ante-natal care, ecstatic birthing, and consciously tactile and loving parenting.

Given our children do survive perinatally and into childhood then they need to learn. Children are voracious learning machines that live in an intense learning state. Children learn through play and emulation. Children watch everything, copy everything and explore everything

through role play and creative play. Children don't develop a rational and abstracting mind fully until they are about 7-8 years old.
Before this age they inhabit very emotional and magical perspectives on the world where they are exploring patterns, relationships, identities and nuances of the world around them. Hence the necessary role of stories, art and myth in children early years education.
Some styles of education try to teach children by rote before the necessary brain development has occurred. Rote learning of reading, writing and religion appear to prohibit active and creative learning.
I question then whether we are more interested in filling our children with our own views on religion, work, money, life and love than truly facilitating their learning.
I view early years religious education, where specific beliefs about the nature of reality, connection and causation are foisted on children, as a form of psycholgical child abuse.
We appear more interested in passing down our personal mythology of connection rather than allowing children to explore the world of human belief and find out for themselves how they experience connection, understand reality and vision causation.
I do not believe religion should be taught in schools or have anything to do with schooling at all.
We could simply teach 'the fascinating world of human belief'. That way we might even give our children the possibility of being belief artists, rather than dogmatists, fundamentalists and closed hearted, frightened bigots. If religion really offers anything useful it will survive.

Real learning allows children to respond freely and creatively to the future conditions they will face, future conditions we cannot even begin to apprehend. We don't know what the future holds, we really don't, so imposing what we feel children need on to them, is wasting and disregarding their unconditioned creative and responsive skills.

The hypothalamic pituitary adrenal axis (HPAA) is the line of midbrain and glands through the core of the body that gives us our basic tones of response to life pressures.
These glands control metabolism, immune function, stress response, control of fluids and minerals, sexual response and more.
The response thresholds of this HPAA are set up in the first six-months of life according to the conditions we are born into, is it stress rich or

relatively stress free? The thresholds of response of the HPAA informs our future perspectives and responsive patterns. Our basic tone of response to stressful scenarios is set up early.
The physical and emotional holding of babies, communication with babies, and the level of loving physical contact a baby receives, all affect how this HPAA is set up and how the brain develops.
Lower thresholds of stress response, set as a default in infancy, prepare for the probability of a life lived in a stressed state.
All the complex relationship issues and disease possibilities that arise with a low threshold of stress response then follow.
A brain growing in a poverty of touch has more stress hormones in it and the various parts of the brain do not join up as successfully, they don't and cant' communicate with each other as well.
Babies and children up to the age of 7-8 cannot emotionally self-regulate at all or very well. This we learn through having it done to us through holding, touch and example. Parents who expect their babies to deal with their feelings before the child is capable of such responsibility, or get reflexively stressed at the emotional responses of their children because of their own inability to emotionally self-regulate (they were mistreated by their parents), are teaching the children to emotionally dysregulate. They are setting their children up with all the stress based disease possibilities that we know stress leads to.

Childhood adversity is the biggest cause of stress and disease, the biggest contributor to health budgets, social service budgets, educational difficulties and criminal justice budgets in the world.
If we could learn how to manage our children according to how their brains actually grow and not according to some cultural, political or religious agenda on childcare our societies would radically change.
We build cortisol rich, dysfunctional brains in our children with a low threshold HPAA through ignorance of how brains grow, our own unresolved childhood trauma from awkward upbringing, un-love, neglect and abuse.

Cortiol is the hormonal mediator of long term stress and in growing brains, excess cortisol prevents the neurons growing properly and prohibits bits of the brain communicating effectively with each other.

Cortisol toxified brains cannot maximise the synaptic connections,

faster brain channels and communicative capacities between brain regions available to brains grown in more cortisol free childhoods.
It is this possibility of clearer communication between brain regions that is the key difference between a stressed, emotionally reactive baby and child than a more relaxed, relatively cortisol free, spaciously creative baby and child.

Cortisol rich brains also grow with less pleasure receptors. What use is pleasure when we are trying to just survive?
Experiencing less pleasure, as well as being less cognitively adept, less emotionally intelligent and less intellectually responsive cannot be described as a quality lifestyle.
Why would we do this to millions of our children globally?

Maybe to make them into willing factory fodder, or emotionally numbed troopers willing to fight the next battle on behalf of merchant bankers masquerading as patriots?

Or am I just being cynical?

We facilitate a relaxed HPAA in an infant, with its brain that maximises its potential neuronal connections and accentuates it's myelin sheaths which speed up neuronal traffic, through loving touch, being held, positive communication and being surrounded by loving, unstressed and joyful relatives.
Now we have to ask how we create loving, unstressed and joyful relatives?

We look at gross national happiness and quality of life measurements rather than Gross National Product and economic measures of profit as the arbiter of what a good life is.
Literally planetary wellbeing, ecologically and socially and people's wellbeing, emotionally and physically has to come before profit and dividends or we are destroying our children's future. This doesn't mean no profit, it means profit is put into it's correct place, third. Planet (and its myriad species) first, people second and profit third.

Neurologically authentic and intelligently applied living-body based yogic practices, practices of mindfulness and meditation, psychothera-

py at functional relational depth and loving community can, potentially, reset the HPAA, build new pleasure receptors, and craft new neurological connections that may have been absent previously. This is the nature of the self-applied neuroplasticity, which is what the somatically intelligent movement practices, meditation and mindfulness, re-wilding and the community focused practices I teach are about.
However, why do the rehabilitation when prevention is possible?

What would we rather have for our children?

A happy life or a decade or two of therapeutic engagement so they can manage a sustainable relationship if they're lucky?

The level of therapeutic practice required to rebuild the HPAA and craft sustainable relationship is not small. If one is devoted to somatic, emotional, cognitive and vibrational awareness practices, as well as a therapeutic relationship, it can be possible to achieve such reconditioning of the nervous system over a number of years. A person also has to be fortunate enough to come across teachings and practices that facilitate such change, and sadly this is not as common as it could yet be, especially in the increasing commercialisation and profit focus of the modern presentation of such practices.

Watching children grow, I'm fascinated by their sparkling intelligence at very early ages. Our culture tells us that children are empty brains ready for conditioning, ready to be filled with information. Parenting tells me that children are wonderfully responsive and creative beings whose bright intelligence informs every single interaction they have. Babies are so communicative that they create body and sound languages from a very early age, languages that only their close caring family will understand.
I remember my little ones asking for water with eye gaze and gestures and their response when that message was understood. Once the message was understood it could be used as a preverbal language for my child to get its hydration needs met on demand from the child's agency rather than mine. In this way the child is learning of its own needs and communicative power in the field of relational responsivity from a very early age. If I had failed to pay attention because I was too caught up in my own difficult neurochemicals, or uninterested in my child's behav-

iours, because of my belief that it was an unformed and uncommunicative, then my child would never have been responded to in a way that gave veracity to its early search for communicative agency.
If these communications are missed, the child will, with the inattention it receives, shut down its sparkling genius. If a child's endeavours to communicate are consistently missed or ignored it will not make the synaptic connections that grow its brain. These potential and real connections reflect the relational and communicative genius every baby and child is, and we all are. It is these key love-relationships that teach the child who it is, it is a relational being, it learns about itself and knows itself through and as relationship, as we all do.

Parents who are too busy, or unable to see their child's communicative attempts, due, perhaps, to their own insensitivity or too stressed (caught up in their own difficult neurochemicals) to pay attention effectively, miss these vital developmental opportunities for their children. Parents who hand over their children to carers, even to the most highly trained of nursery staff, mostly miss this vital opportunity for their children. Nursery staff simply cannot pay the same loving attention in the way that a parent, saturated with oxytocin, dopamine and other neurotransmitters of love and attention, can. Nursery staff cannot be expected to tune into each individual child's micro-developmental language, this is unreasonable, especially if they are looking after many children. In such environments, even with the best will in the world, the children can slowly shut their synaptic possibilities down from the absence of the appreciative, responsive gaze of the significant adults in their life. It is of course usually mother, father, grandparents or older siblings who are the significant adults, and who most deeply understand the child. Conversely, some children may benefit from the care of skilled nursery staff if their home environment is toxic and their primary carers are uncaring.
But, why would any parent miss such a special time for themselves and their children?

Does the maximisation of profit really warrant an emotionally ignorant culture?

What a crying shame for parents, children and culture.
My belief is that this is a special time for both parents. My children

where never in my womb, I don't have one! I sang and chanted to them in the womb and with the scientific evidence that pre-natal learning is a reality, this was a good thing to do, as it predisposed my children to know my voice when they were born. This allowed me to look after them and soothe them when they were very little. I had to develop my good relations with my little children through time, contact and involvement. If I had been a distant, stressed out authority figure busy trying to make more profit, this opportunity for a profound depth of loving relationship with my children would have been completely missed. So, this time is not just down to the mother, it is ideally both parents, in loving harmony.

Men have to retrain their testosterone from the conditioned patterns of cultural testosterone tales (heroism, warfare, corporate battles and investment banking) into whole new ways, because this is what our evolutionary context requires.

When a culture understands that all children are its children, that we are all in it together and that all our children are our future, then maybe there will be positive change in terms of honouring and prioritising childcare over profit.

We understand the stages of child development very well.

We also have models of education from many sources, each of which has strengths and weaknesses. Some specialise in creativity and being comfortable in nature, others teach effectively about mathematics but lack exposure to myth and creativity. Some focus on project learning or pattern recognition. Some styles of education appear to focus more on systems of measurement of a child's supposed abilities, rather than be concerned about the child's actual development. Others appear to be driven by political, religious or corporate agendas.

We also know that a dollar spent in childhood on effective and affective education and prevention of childhood adversity is worth thousands and thousands of dollars spent later on education, health care, social services, criminal justice and rehabilitation programmes.

So, if we are to co-create and co-evolve a new world and enlightening education then prioritising resources towards neurologically effective childcare and education is important. Finding the strengths in each educational approach and each individual child, will offer us a comprehensive and broad approach to the education we can offer our future generations.

Education that invites creativity; comfort, presence and relationship with wild nature; effective development in mathematics, science and literacy; pattern recognition; cognitive skills; emotional literacy and intelligence; somatic intelligence and spatial skills; meditative brain training; as well as exploring the new arising boundaries of our carbon-silicon interface in a good way, can all be brought into our education for the future.

Understanding neurological development and neuroplasticity, we might prioritise skills that lead to balanced brain development. Balanced brain development would most probably include the following thirty-two areas to help our children realise their full potential.

- Child centred, project based explorations
- Appropriate touch
- Subject/object relations and core identity
- Communication skills
- Self-esteem
- Intra-personal skills
- Interpersonal skills
- Appreciation
- Creativity
- Deep ecological relations with our ecosphere
- Critical thinking
- Basic life skills, including creating beautiful food and self-care
- Numeracy and mathematics
- Literacy
- Other languages
- Somatic intelligence, body skills and body appreciation
- Spatial intelligence
- Musical intelligence
- Understanding and working with their own mind through mindfulness and meditative mind training
- Emotional intelligence
- Self-directed learning skills
- Ecological intelligence and connection with wild nature

- Explorations and creativity in human belief
- Global citizenship, rights and responsibilities
- Understanding science, making good science
- Exploring global history from a range of viewpoints
- Exploring the world of human belief and the power of belief
- Information technology and exploration of our car bon-silicon interface
- Central nervous system management skills
- Wellbeing psychology
- Culture co-creation
- Conscious co-evolution

Some educational analysts would add financial intelligence. However in our future enlightened economy, maximising profit and accumulating personal wealth will be of minimal consequence.
Cultivating, developing and giving one's greatest gifts and facilitating the full potential of all whilst generating quality of life for all will be what life is about.
Flowing into conscious co-evolution, aware of this key-point, we will be finding clear ways to help the next generation be prepared to meet the changing conditions they will face.
The world will be as it is, we have no real way of knowing what that might be, beyond guesswork, intuition and belief, and this is not enough.
By preparing our children, helping them to learn to learn, build creativity, develop critical thinking and the other thirty-two skills of potential, they will be more likely to know what to do and how to deal with the changes they face.

The sign of intelligence is not knowing what to do when we know what to do, the sign of intelligence is working out what to do when we don't know what to do.
This is what we want for our children, isn't it?

After all childcare and education really is the key to the future.

What else do you feel would facilitate healthy, holistic child-centred learning that will prepare our future generations in the best way?

Compassion

the eighth key to conscious co-evolution is compassion

Invertebrates, fish, amphibians and reptiles do not emote, they have no developed emotional brain. They have nervous systems that feel gratification or satisfaction and of course they experience pain and seek prevention or withdrawal from this possibility. These two basic drives of the separate feeling nervous system, moving towards what is perceived as desirable and away from what is perceived as threatening are common to all of life.

Plants sense and move with light, they are phototropic. Plants also sense and respond to gravity, they are geotropic. Plants sense vibration, emit vibration and have tactile senses. Plants also communicate through complex underground root, mycorhizzal, and bio-chemical communicative systems, plants are sentient. Plants communicate with each other and grow towards positive stimuli and away from toxic stimuli.

All of life has these two basic drives that yogic psychology speaks of as raga and dvesha, craving and aversion.These two primary drives are the foundation of the self-sense, the locus of identity.
Humans also have a third drive, a third way our self-sense makes sense of the world and defines our world and this 'ego' drive is moha in Sanskrit or 'ignorant indifference' in English.
Living beings seek to draw some things into themselves and push others away. We've mentioned these previously, but it's our ignorant indifference that really defines whether we should grace ourselves with the titles homo ignoramus or homo sapiens.
Humans, failing to pay attention to the reality of inseparability, the fact that everything is seamlessly connected, behave as if they are disconnected from everything else and treat events, experiences, nature and planet as well as other people as if they are irrelevant, this is ignorant indifference.

More primitive life-forms, as mentioned, do not have the brain structure to feel and experience emotions in the way we do. We humans love to anthropomorphise all creatures, especially the furry ones. We make other beings behave as if they were humans in our mind. This is the world according to Pixar and Disney.

Many birds and all mammals exhibit the brain structures for emotional bonding and the navigation of the world of intra-specific relationship through emotion.
Fishes and reptiles, however, often eat their own children, mammals and more advanced birds more rarely do so. They will, however, eat each other's children. For example, male tigers will kill the children of another male when they take over a new female.

Cetaceans, whales and dolphins have been around for twenty-eight million years and have brains with much greater coalescence between the emotional and cognitive aspects. They probably do not separate emotion and cognition in the way we tend too, but then they also don't use tools so have a different relationship with abstraction and creative process in that way. The world of sonar gives them a whole way of feeling into the world that we don't have and as a result their brains may be much more set up for intra-group communication than ours.

As moderately advanced primates we've been around as a separate species for 2 million years or less, depending how you define our separation from our hominid cousins the Neanderthals, Denisovans and Florensians.
Our brains, which are still in the process of evolution, have emotional capacities to feel connected or disconnected, to empathise or not and to feel compassion and love or not. Brains are not separate from bodies and emotions are experienced in the body, sounds obvious but its worth pointing out, as many still believe bodies and brains are separate things.

Long-term meditators, who have been tested with brain scanning devices, evidence brains that can work differently to folk who have never meditated or developed awareness and compassion practices.
The left pre-frontal cortex and executive centres are more fully active in meditators. The emotional centres are more regulated and emotional responses are responses not reflexes. Higher levels of the brain wave

pattern called gamma-synergy, appear to be more active in regular meditators who also evidenced greater levels of compassion. Gamma-synergy may well be a neuro-correlate of the seamless experience of deep ecological connection across the fractal boundaries of self and environment, cognition and emotion, brains and body, mind and cosmos that some people call 'enlightenment'. Gamma synergy may well be what yogis call 'citta vrtti nirodha', the cessation of the fluctuating waves of the thinking-feeling level of consciousness.

So what about compassion?

Compassion arises naturally from this gamma-synergy state of seamless knowing. Until then we build the muscles of compassion through practice. Compassion practice is an evolutionary art.

Compassion practice when matched by compassionate behaviour also leads into the non-dual, gamma synergy state, from which compassion arises naturally.

Lets consider feelings related to compassion...

- Sympathy is a feeling of pity or sorrow for someone else's misfortune.

- Empathy is the ability and behaviour of both understanding and sharing the feelings of another. It's like being able to feel into their skin and know how something really is for them.

- Compassion is the ability of understanding another's situa tion, sharing the feelings, coupled with appropriate action and behaviour to facilitate as much positive change in their situation as is possible for you and that other person, whilst you remain, centred in grace.

There is a possible development, a progression of understanding and action in the realisation of inseparability through the process of these three emotional states. Compassion is more advanced than empathy, which is more developed than sympathy.

Compassion is a skill-set. There have been many different measures and scales of moral behaviour and development proposed by psychologists. They all consider moral development to be founded in treating and behaving towards other beings with mutual regard.

A morally developed brain behaves differently to a more selfishly functioning brain. A compassionate person appears to be happier than a selfish person, according to a number of studies of the effects of compassion on the human brain.

Compassion is also evidenced to make you more attractive to others, broaden your perspectives and generate greater wisdom, make you healthier and less likely to get diseases. Compassion is natural and doesn't work if it is forced, though it can be entrained through practice.

Compassion is also infectious and spreads through communities. You can be an agent of change simply be being kind to others.

There is a common mistake with regard to what compassion means in terms of one's daily practice and life in the world though. Compassion is not about seeking cartoon happy endings for everybody, not just about everybody getting their fair slice of cream cake. This style of compassion doesn't recognise that everything is impermanent flow, that everything is empty of inherent separate existence, that every 'thing' dies. Cartoon style compassion wants to cuddle everything and turn the whole world into fluffy teddy bears, care bears, popsicles and unicorns. This, though quite sweet at its best, can be nauseating at its neoliberal worst, and can be helpfully understood as 'idiot compassion'.

Real compassion recognises that all things change, that all apparently separate beings die and that there is no separate intrinsic existence to any apparently separate being. It is from this basis in 'reality' that real compassion begins.

So, real compassion seeks to actively reduce unnecessary pain, whilst recognising that pain is an inevitable consequence of residence as a nervous system. Real compassion seeks to help all beings understand that suffering is entirely optional. This is where real compassion becomes so powerful because it means we can choose to do something about suffering, we can eliminate it from our own experience and we can help and encourage others to do the same. Real compassion then

becomes a co-evolutionary act.
How do we eliminate suffering?

We stop inhabiting the separate self-story as if it were the deepest truth of our existence.

The self-construct can be usefully viewed as a neurological contraction of our possibilities. This neurological event positively serves as a vehicle to navigate the experience of form, and the appearance of separation.

At its worst, the self-construct becomes our most cherished identity, one that requires defence, defiance, justification, and an aggressive modus operandi in the world to get what 'I' need, to satisfy 'My' feelings and enlarge, defend and control that territory which is 'Mine'.
And, in this process of 'self' aggrandisement, never mind anyone else, unless they are also 'mine', my friends, my family, my country, my religion, my, my, mine.
And, even then if they cross me I will be merciless in my psychopathic behaviour to eliminate them as a threat to my ego progression!
This is the unresolved shadow side of the 'self' or if you prefer 'self-oriented' or 'selfish' construct. It's all about me and my world, me and my story.

Living as a self-construct in the world of impermanent flow is tediously unsatisfactory.
We can never truly win, never finally possess, and never really be safe unless we eventually get that we are nobody, we are not that darned self-construct after all.

When we know that we are not this neurological fantasy, this contraction, then we don't need to defend or attack or justify in that same old way.

When we embrace that each of us is deliciously riddled with feelings, that we are all rather tentative about dying, that we're all vulnerable, we can begin to be compassionate.

Real happiness and joy can only begin when the relentless dissatisfaction of the grasping, shoving, withdrawing, fearful and indifferent ignorance of the self-contraction is seen for what it always was - an evolutionary phase and neurological fantasy, one that facilitated a particular period of human development that we're now rapidly co-evolving beyond.

Since we mention development, idiot compassion would have every being seen as developmentally equal. We're not. Real compassion sees the developmental level of any individual as appropriate and also therefore capable of development.

Human potential is possible from the eyes of compassion, but not from the eyes of idiot compassion that sees everyone as if we were all existing on a kind of two dimensional flatland. Everyone is equal in essence but not necessarily in terms of development.
This is part of our beauty. I'm really not very developed at playing guitar, I have a lot to learn, and in amny other areas as well, i assure you!

Real compassion also knows that we can only see and know from the perspective we currently occupy, so at the right time, in the right way, real compassion, however it moves, lovingly offers the developmental medicine as opportunities, invitations and contexts for each of us as individuals to facilitate our own development.

Real compassion helps us grow beyond all versions of holding a position in space-time, so that we can all become nobody. Compassion is also the stick of Zen, the cancer that eats our body, the prison sentence and whatever it is that helps us see our inconsequence, our fragility, our vulnerability and through this our beauty and everyeone's beauty.

I recommend becoming nobody and nothing, become inconsequential. Only now can we see and know that all beings are equal in essence and potential. All beings can develop and move from 'Buddhas to Be' out of their contraction, pain and suffering, leaving behind the distorted influences around which they built their self-contraction and self-story and finally be awakened ones.

Real compassion leads this journey into inevitable inconsequence and is the force of consciousness moving through the affective aspect of inseparability. It is unfolding as awareness.

So, what has love got to do with it?

Love is such a loaded word, partly because it means so many things to so many people. Love has correlations from loving ice-cream through to unbearable passion for a lover, and to the feeling of a vast benevolent universe as a function of some creative principle.

Both compassion and love require some quality of presence, they are both facets of being fully here, now, present and spacious. Ideally they are both aware of all the ramifications through space-time of each and every thought, feeling and action. This is what presence implies.
Love and compassion is the feeling of presence, it is the feeling aspect of pristine awareness.

Authentic compassion is the direct experience of developmental understanding and appropriate action to relieve unnecessary pain.

Authentic compassion seeks to resolve suffering and facilitate the movement of all beings into the intelligent dissolution and transcension of the self-contraction, so that each being discovers their natural state as awakened presence, moving in the world as love and compassion.

Love and compassion is the deepest feeling-wisdom of inseparability. Compassion is a key aspect of conscious co-evolution.

Compassion is the active recognition of indivisibility, and it is the eighth key to conscious co-evolution.

Cultivating Pleasure

the ninth key to conscious co-evolution is cultivating pleasure

The clitoris is the only organ that we know of, in the whole of evolutionary history solely devoted to pleasure.

The clitoris is not just a nerve rich button sitting above a woman's vagina. It's also the deep structure rooted through into the G-spot, the vulva and the vaginal walls as a Yoniweb, a veritable matrix of nerves and erectile tissue, a multi-limbed structure all evolved to facilitate pleasure, ecstatic bliss, power and creativity.

The nerves in the glans penis of the male are less in number and more localised to the tip of the penis, though the analogous erectile tissue is obviously present.

For pornographers and those that have the misfortune to have their emotions numbed and the connections between genitals and heart closed, through believing cultural lies or through fear and ignorance, sexuality is a matter of friction and gratification. Sexuality is just something one person does to another, a matter of turgid flesh, juices and pumping meat, something you can buy, sell and control.
Why do we let our younger genrations be educated in sexuality by these pornographers?

Through religious inculcation of shame and fear of sexuality we have effectively abdicated from responsibility for effective education around this key area of our human co-evolution. The consequence is our younger generations being taught the emotionally numb, pumping meat version of pleasure and sexuality.

Through yoga of the living body (somatic yoga), breath work, meditation, sexual yogas and loving relationship (with self and/or other/s) we can know sexuality to be a profound sharing of energy, love, bliss and

profound blessings.
We know, through our practice, that the feelings of pleasure and bliss arising through the genitals can be extended into the totality of the physical, energetic and emotional bodies and beyond by using the breath and the mind. We know that the illusion of self and other can be dissolved into the bliss focused recognition of the two as one, the two being whole and holy.

What has this got to do with conscious co-evolution?

In most animals the procreative act is a time of great danger, both male and female are vulnerable and potential lunch. In gorillas, for example, the penis contains a bone to facilitate rapid ejaculation from the relatively small penis and the basic drive in most animals is to squirt and run.
Biological sexual drives are innate and serve to combine gametes as quickly as possible, and get back to the business of eating. As the joke about some men's sexuality goes, it's like the panda - eats, shoots and leaves.

Our core line brings us into vulnerable ventral surface to ventral surface connection and communication. The development of the clitoris in human females, along with the possibilty of face-to-face mating and the development of language, allows and invites a whole new realm of pleasurable possibility well beyond the emotionally numb, pumping meat version of pleasure and sexuality.

For sure the essential genetic drives are always the same, to deliver seeds from the male, receive seeds into the female and incubate the next generation.
However, with the ascendancy of the human species we now also have the opportunity to celebrate the sexual act as a means of cultivating and sharing ecstatic pleasure, bliss, connection and the realisation of inseparability.

The sexual act, devoid of emotional integrity, has been used as a political tool of domination and control. Various abuses such as shame, guilt, propaganda, witch burning, stoning, media portrayals, and genital mutilation have been, and still are, the means exercised by politicised religions to destroy the beauty, power and validity of loving sexuality as

a form of love, worship and realisation. These abuses have been used to control women's power, creativity and freedom.
So, we're talking about polar opposite experiences using the same process - sexuality. One is loving and co-evolutionary, the other abusive, oppressive and controlling.
What are dogmatic patriarchal (or kiriarchal) religions so scared of?

All patriarchal and kiriarchal religions have sought to control women, women's sexuality and reproductive capacity, and prioritise the descent of property through the male line. Men can also be unnerved and disturbed by women's powerful sexual drives and women's immense capacity for orgasm, bliss and connection.

Throughout modern history men have evidenced fear of the yoni and/or a desire to control and destroy its power. Yoni is a sanskrit word that describes women's genitalia in a positive light. Yoni means the source of life and covers the whole womens reproductive anatomy and her relationship to the cosmos. Another word is Kund, meaning 'holy well' as the source of life. Kunda puspa is a powerful term for menstruation, it means the flowers of the holy well. This is despite the mysogny and control towards mentstruating women evident now in the lands where this word comes from. Kund is also where we get the Germanic word Gecynd from. Gecynd is the root of the words kin as in family, kind as in both our species and compassionate behaviour, clan as in tribe and also cunt. The word cunt has been abused in the west to diminish women and women's anatomy to an expletive. The power of menstration has been diminished to 'the curse'. The name for the female organs of pleasure, reproduction and birth have been reduced down to vagina, meaning a hole. Such is the psychological field of abuse women have to grow in and live in and in which we are working to readdress the ludicrous imbalance evident in the modern world.

Control of women has been done through the endless permutations of misogyny, previously mentioned. In the contemporary western world it's happening through grotesque objectification, where what matters most about a woman is clearly not her art, her mind, or her life but the shape of her body. Please look at any tabloid newspaper to see this acted out in front of your eyes.

Bearing all of this in mind - if a child grows up in adverse and stressful situations then one of the brain's responses to these conditions is to reduce the number of pleasure receptors. Pleasure receptors grow better in brains that have developed in environments of ease, acceptance, love, tactile holding, emotional contact and celebration. The capacity to feel and enjoy pleasure deeply is the result of a well developed brain.

For those who's brains are deficient in pleasure receptors, pleasure focused practices or sadhanas, such as massage and erotic exploration can be highly beneficial to re-establish the brain's riches of natural pleasure receptors, this is one of the roles of western neo-tantra.
How can a brain closed to ordinary levels of endorphins be expected to open in ecstatic bliss?

So, pleasure can be skilfully, tenderly and lovingly used as a therapeutic tool to facilitate a more pleasure receptive brain and a higher quality of life.

There's a big difference between pleasure in service of the ego, as basic hedonism and self-gratification, versus pleasure as a tool of service to allow an individual's neurology to open to love and bliss as a means of transcending the self-structure.

Loving sexuality can be a way to blow one open to bliss-emptiness, to realisation of the interconnected seamless whole. I personally, through direct experience, know this as true, and trust you will, or of course already do. Your'e welcome to read my book The Way of Desire, if you want to go into the psychology of awakening with explicit exploration and utilisation of erotic energy and sensual delight as part of the path of awakening.
There's a big difference between lust divorced from love, and love spiced by the raw juiciness of lust. Lust for waking up to what's real is why we're on the path of conscious co-evolution.

Flowers hanging off the trees in springtime are the genitals of plants, we give them, unconsciously perhaps, as symbols of love and beauty. Yet, many people see their own and others genitalia with shame, guilt and as symbols of disgust with basic bodily function.
How have we got into such a cultural pickle?

What a bizarre conundrum. This can change, even though the old paradigm of body-negative feeling, shame, guilt and distorted thinking still dominates much of the global world-view. Our culture is historically riddled with…

- Oppressive religious conditioning
- Disrespect, objectification and control of women
- Pathological conditioning of men
- Disrespect for women's choices
- Teaching young people about sexuality through ignorance and por nography
- Criminalisation of aspects of sexual exploration and expression
- Predominance of pain, punishment and suffering over the neurology of pleasure and bliss
- Irresponsible mating where people pay no real attention to the consequences of their behaviour

We now seek difference.
Loved up, loving and physically aware intimate contact cultivates deeper awareness and celebration of the somatic-emotional relationships with our fellow beings.
Engaging like this encourages the co-creation and awakening of respectful and mutually consenting relationship.
Authentic love and freedom has no taboos other than skilful behaviour. Skilful behaviour doesn't harm the awakening of ourselves or other beings. From this view, all conscious behaviours promote loving, consenting behaviour, fuel for finding the presence of awareness in and as the ground of all.

Loving, mutual sexuality consists of all of the following...

- Clear and open communication
- Beautiful lust
- Physical play
- Fun
- Mutual respect
- Creative sexual expression
- Deep listening
- Heart opening love
- Blissful ecstatic openness to the other

- Full responsibility for all our thoughts, feelings and behaviours
- Full honouring of all parties involved.
- Consenting adults, willing to explore, with awareness through sexuality, desire and love.
- Finding the expressions and experience of union.
- Does your dynamic affect the world around you? If it is harm ing others in any way, take full responsibility and change what you are doing, rapidly.
- Loving aware sexuality as open and celebratory is a necessity for con scious co-evolution.
- Reclaiming touch, sensuality and loving sexuality as a valid and powerful approach to finding the presence of awareness in everyday life.
- Cultivating conscious relationship, playfulness, energetic explora tion and a lived expression of love as a crucial practice in our gender befuddled, prurient, and overly commercial culture.
- Part of the way we celebrate being fully alive and experiencing the essential flow of life-force.
- Maintaining the right to say 'No', the prerogative to change our minds and stop.
- Consent as an ongoing process, necessary in each moment and from moment to moment. This is an aspect of clear and attentive commu nication that provides a loving foundation for relationship.
- Know each other as equal in love.
- Whatever your sexual orientation and however you choose to lovingly engage and explore is up to you.
- Constant letting go, a constant non-gripping of any moment or any experience.

Bliss-emptiness, as the essence of awareness in relationship to all arising phenomena is found through the inner work. The inner work teaches us that all nervous system sensations are empty in and of themselves, they are just vibrational flow.

Empty doesn't mean void, devoid or nothingness, empty is just empty of conceptual limitation, empty of self-sense, empty of definition, empty of emptiness.

Empty is therefore totally full of possibility. Emptiness is the essence of form, everything we sense and perceive and form is none other than emptiness.

When we know this, through the inner work, we can understand what love means.
When we get this, all our actions are response-able, in alignment with what is, and are the greatest expression of what is, no harm is caused. So when we know all our nervous system sensations as empty, they can all be felt, seen, tasted for what they are and left to move. Nothing is grasped, as there is no one to do the grasping and nothing to be grasped. There is only flow.

Practices of lovemaking can then be offered in sacrifice, as we resolves our neurological separation, our self-sense, and each other's into bliss-emptiness.
The energy of orgasm and bliss is then cultivated, spread throughout our energy field and expanded out into the universe with no boundaries as we dissolve.

Conscious co-evolution celebrates loving committed relationship, where consorts can deepen in intimacy over time. In this way we mirror each other's shadow and facilitate awakening for each other. We become each other's teacher.

Whether you engage with a single consort in intimate embrace or choose to co-create loving scenarios where the appearance of monogamy is not the norm is up to you. Most people find that being deeply successful at intimacy in monogamy is required first, otherwise the tendency is to slide into non-heart focused lovemaking, a masquerade of intimacy that is really some sort of sexual addiction or bliss chase. Most people find monogamy hard enough, and polyamory (or macroamory as I prefer to call it) even harder, it it is not to descend into sexual selfishness and dys-intimacy.

Continuously learning, learning what it is to balance the rich passion of erotic love with compassion and the experience of universal love, we can explore the wealth of being alive as consciously sexual, consciously loving, highly aware beings, rising and expanding in love as love.

Switch On...
Switched on lovers honour each other. Totally! Worship at the bio-philiac shrine of the holy life breath, dancing heart, sparkling mind, pulsing

emotions and juicy genitals in conjunction with the aligned left-prefrontal cortex.

Switched on lovers bow, kiss, and dance in bliss in each mundane moment... to all of totality. Aroma and fragrance becomes sweet as each opens in love as love and all bodily flows are known as holy. Taste is pure delight as we know what we taste is the one taste of divinity, Ekarasa.

Switched on lovers know that what we see as the shape, curve, wrinkle and line is the landscape of love as story... As the play of time and space, the divine as flow.

Switched on lovers know one as two, two as one, each in all, the all as each, as reality.
Breath, energy flows and mind, seamless as each others story dissolves into bliss, as this moment of love is life loving itself, as us.

Switched on, simply refuse to do duality, it's the pit of duality or it's life as love. This choice arises in each moment… and is met with delight, clarity and joy. We choose reality, the inseparable, over our story.

Switched on, we see the whole phenomenal world as our lover, always rising and expanding in love.

Wild and free, evolving conscious, co-evolving, responsible and aware. Co-evolving through self-reflection, self-realisation and the bio-philiac wonder of manifold life, life loving itself, dancing as itself in Presence-Being.

Conscious co-evolution has three strands of realisation, one being focus, the second being weaving and the third being 'getting it'.

Focus is…

Focus is the practice of cultivating realisations of impermanence, inter-dependence and emptiness. This requires psycho-emotional clarity be maximised, and engagements and distractions minimised, so that one can deeply compute these three realisations through the cultivation of focus.

The Three Realisations…

1) Impermanence - means that physical existence is limited, death can occur at any time, termination will happen. The first stage of realisation is to really 'get' this truth and live with this recognition embedded in our neurology and our lives. It offers a certain vulnerability that gives a space for more authentic relationship.

If we stop pretending we are physically immortal and engage with life from this place of honest fragility and vulnerability, our inter-relating is so much more intimate. If we wait to die before we recognise the blindingly obvious its a bit late!

The compassion in our heart that arises and radiates from the recognition of this unguarded truth allows deeper human intimacy and less pretence. There are no winners in impermanence.

2) Inter-dependence - the living systemic gnosis that no-thing in this flow is separate from any other thing. Every-thing is visibly or invisibly intertwined, we just have to look closely enough. All 'things' are really only appearances. What this means is that nothing in itself has any solid, permanent, defined or separate existence, it's all patterns, vortices of energy. What we view as solid 'reality' is scintillating shades of the continuum of matter (as vortices of energy) and flowing energy such as we find in the electro-magnetic spectrum, both at the same time.

This living systemic quantum-ecology requires that we share our contributions with the world in a more cohesive and less brutal way. We are no longer the dominators or owners of the planet, we are part of the flow of life, where independence is known to be illusory.

3) Empty-fullness - knowing there is no inherent, separate, continuous, defined or permanent existence to any-thing, including our bodies, feelings, thoughts, self-sense, pleasure, pain and so on. When we look deeply into any-thing, we find no-thing solid. Nothing exists in itself, of it-self, all we find is no-thing.
This is what 'emptiness' means.
Every-thing is empty-full. Empty-fullness is every-thing and yet it cannot be found.
What is there that is not empty of any separate inherence?

When what is empty is everything, is not everything full?

The empty is the full and the full is the empty. There is nothing anywhere we can name since everything is a fractal, seamless play of energy and appearances.
There are no names, nouns become partial verbs to describe facets of the flow of fullness.
There are no senses nor sense organs since all the senses and sense organs are simply ways of translating the field of vibration, flowing as appearances into the illusion of solidity to enable biological continuity.

Getting empty-fullness is a result of looking deeply through focus.
It is from the base of these realisations that weaving begins. Weaving grows out of focus.

Weaving Is...
Weaving as the path to awakening is through the earthy and raw vitality of the flow principle.

The body, the flows of energy, emotion and thought that constitute our world of appearances are the flow principle.

Because we begin where we are, we find the balance to the flow principle by giving into flow. We cannot find the balance to flow through seeking stillness or centre. Stillness or centre, the awareness principle arises by going into flow and through flow, not around it, above it or by ignoring it.

To find sentience or the awareness principle we explore energy, movement and space-time through body based practices, feeling based practices, exploration of mind and who we are through meditativce practices and more, this is the inner work.

Conscious co-evolution depends on our capacity to be with flow, in flow and drop beyond flow into clear awareness, within which, through which flow flows.

You cannot have weaving without threads, one needs focus and mind training to work with conscious co-evolution. Otherwise it's like trying to read a book without learning one's ABC. Conscious co-evolution is much more than pleasure and sexuality, way bigger than being defined by the flow principle alone.

However, the flow principle is really important in conscious co-evolution as it is the path. This is the crux, the path to know totality and one's original nature of awareness is the flow principle, this is the high road to subjective depth.

Totality can be visioned as the ecstatic balance of masculine and feminine principles, the flow and the awareness principles. But flow is the way home to this.

Interestingly, Indian Tantra and Tibetan Tantra work with the masculine and feminine principles in apparent opposition and contradiction. Indian Tantra has consciousness, the awareness principle as the male and energy, form and flow as the female principle of space and movement.
Tibetan Tantra has the feminine principle as awareness and wisdom, as the pregnant emptiness that is the source of everything. The masculine principle in Tibetan Tantra is method. Method arises out of form and flow, it is a function of space, time and movement and involves effort. Method is sadhana and is male.

So we can see that masculine and feminine principles in this sense are not fixed 'truths' but human focused perspectives, teaching metaphors and methods of approach to the direct experience of the totality, from the illusion of separation and the expereince of gender polarity.

So, in conscious co-evolution we take out the gender, though this is fun to work with in visualisations and such, and talk about the flow principle (feminine) and the awareness principle (masculine).

Conscious co-evolution and sexuality

Osho in his time wrote a book titled From Sex to Superconsciousness but as we so rightly know and as I teach, sex is superconsciousness.

Everything is superconsciousness, you cant go from sex to superconsciousness. You can however get from sex as a dance of apparent opposites, as a play of polarities in various states of realisation to realisation of always and already superconsciousness.
Yes, most sex is unrealised, it's not a play of superconsciousness, as a form of devotion and prayer, as a deep recognition of the non-dual. A global movement, knowing that sexuality when 'realised', is prayer, is happening, freeing us from the grip of the culture of guilt and shame.

Realised sexuality is 'worship'. Sex as love, as bliss-emptiness, is and always has been sacred. Diamonds thrown to swine get trampled in the mud, sex in the minds of those living in duality is largely a self-oriented activity of lust, hedonism, pumping meat and personal gratification. It has little to do with approaching reality as superconsciousness, little to do with love.

Focus defines and crafts the threads of realisation, whilst weaving those exquisite threads of realisation into the expansive non-dual tapestry of the always-already reality, as it is.
Superconsciousness is the dance of conscious co-evolution. Conscious co-evolution prepares the body-mind through yoga of the living body, breath work and breath retention, relaxation practice, meditative development and visualisation. All these practices are in the remit of traditional tantra-yoga. Tantra-yoga also traditionally worked with yantra, mantra and nyasa.

Yantra's are geometrical representations of the creative force of the cosmos as a function of light. It is a photonics map and is used as a visualisation tool to understand the photonic end of the vibrational nature of the cosmos, and how we translate vibration through the experience of vision.

Mantra is the sonic energy of the creative force, it is used to understand the cosmos as vibration in the way we translate vibration through audition.

Nyasa or placement is a practice of remembrance. We place vibration, devotion and sacred feeling into the body so it s understood as holistically interwoven with the vibrational matrix, all of which is sacred. Nyasa reminds us of the beauty of the totality and that our bodies are this, it is used to remember the sacredness of existence. It's from this base in traditional tantra-yoga that we can begin to engage in exploring the most powerful energy of all, sexual energy.

When we get that we are not separate existences, but aspects of the flow, we can not just have fun with sexuality but also use it as a powerful tool of awakening, prayer, power and devotion. Pleasure and sexuality are energies that the practitioner of conscious co-evolution can freely engages and play with. Love making practice can also communicate energetically around us as we build, bliss, joy and connection into our system. We make the vibrations of love and communicate those, resonating through our world.

Conscious co-evolution, as the technology of ecstasy, channels sexual energy into love and awakening. This channelling expands sexual energy throughout the whole nervous system, overwhelming it with bliss. Conscious co-evolution, as the technology of ecstasy, channels bliss through the nervous system into the web of fascia and the bio-electric magnetic body. The seamless web of body-mind clarified by yoga of the living body and breath work happens when we activate, energise, strengthen and clarify the flow through all the energy-lines of the body. These primal energies of nature can then roll through our system, expanding the neurological possibilities of bliss to proportions whereby the boundaries between the separate sense-of-self and the flow of energy that is also the cosmos, become totally dissolved into ecstatic surrender as the One, the One that is the many, the many that are the One. "Two become One and the whole is then (known as) holy" as Jivana Kennedy says.

The realisation arising as a result of such practices is the non-dual realisation of the radiant formlessness of totality, pristine awareness, dancing as flow and form.

Weaving the energies of blissful ecstatic embrace through each other's hearts, opening each other's minds to the vast boundless reality and knowing each other as masculine and feminine essence, the awareness and flow principles, in embrace, as the whole cosmos, is profound.

One of the key tools of conscious co-evolution with which we can celebrate and explore reality is pleasure. Pleasure and desire used in this way, as a trans-egoic route to realisation is a path to awakening.

Women as possessors of the finest organ ever evolved for pure pleasure lead the way here as priestess's of bliss. Women have always played this role, which is why patriarchal religions often despise them. Religions of masculist austerity cannot tolerate pleasure as a path or even as an aspect of life, hence fundamentalism in its many mysogynistic flavours is usually brutally ascetic.
As inheritors of a masculist, protestant, pleasure hating culture we may do well to eliminate such stories from our cultural biology, our individual and collective psychology and fully celebrate the union of sexuality, pleasure, bliss and love with emptiness.

However the threads of the three realisations arise, and this is not necessarily through some institutionalised tradition, these threads remain the pre-requisites for the powerful and juicy dance of conscious co-evolution.

These prerequisites have to be authentic realisation, not just thought or imagination. Without these prerequisites a relentless bliss chase for more neurotransmitters occurs. We become nothing more than a junkie to our own neuro-chemicals. Bliss chasing due to it's lack of discipline and authentic realisation has a tendency to head into greater sensation and less sensitivity.
Conscious co-evolution will have us responsible for our own neuro-chemistry, and encourage us to rest in non-contextual bliss and deeper sensitivity and appreciation. Conscious co-evolution includes all aspects of our existence in a rich exploration of the wonderful natural perfection of life.

The third strand…

The third strand is non-dual realisation and living this vision and knowledge of inseparability woven through everyday life as the tapestry of who and how we are in the world.
Seamlessness of awareness is conscious co-evolution, conscious co-evolution is seamless awareness.

Please do enjoy your no-Self and everyone else (as no-Self)... as long as it's mutual and consensual for all parties concerned. So make love as much as you choose, it's a co-evolutionary art-form.

This is the essence of the ninth key to conscious co-evolution.

Commitment and Compersion

commitment and compersion are the tenth key to conscious co-evolution

Commitment

We probably have a biological drive for long term reasonably monogamous relationship. At the same time sixty percent of men and forty-five percent of women in married couples will have affairs.

Fifteen to twenty percent of people in marrioed couples have no or minimal sex. The marriage is a marriage of convenience. People may stay married because they have property together, business together, children together, are scared of being alone or are just happy enough living in habitual non-sexual dynamics.

People in marriages stay together out of convenience because they share the same taboos, both are happy to have no go areas for communication that allow them to remain safe together.

A full fifty percent of first time marriages fail in the U.S.A. More than fifty percent of second marriages fail. A whopping eighty-five percent of relationships fail. So does commitment mean anything?

We probably have a biological drive towards longer term committed monogamous relationship because our children need both adults around for long enough, in a good enough way to achieve maturity with the minimum of psycho-emotional damage.

At the same time we have a tendency towards needing novelty and seeking difference.

Normally in relationship people commit to be faithful, to stay together and to enable each other to deepen in intimacy. Indeed it is deepening in intimacy that probably both devlops and kills relationships. If we

feel safe, because we have some commitment then we can open up in vulnerability and use the relationship as a vehicle to explore our unresolved shadow. For sure those unresolved shadow elements will come out and be visible in relationship anyway. When this happens either we shut down and don't go to the places that trigger the shadows or we seek psychotherapeuti help and explore and ideally resolve our developmental and realtional issues. From here we either grow together or grow apart.
Perhaps if we commited to growth and committed to each others growth, rather than a vision of possession, control and jealousy, at least we would have grounds for amicable separation?

Commitment in relationship is important as it helps us feel safe and allows us to grow. Commitment allows and invites deeper intimacy. Commitment need not be defined by exclusive sexual activity yet if we have sexual engagement outside of the relationship or marriage it usually leads to termination of the couples dynamic.

Jealousy appears to be a deeply hardwired human emotion. Yet if we look at the information we are fed we find the literature on relationship replete with words like 'cheating' and stories of 'jealousy' and crimes of passion.

Reading the works on polyamory where people allow themselves and each other to have initmate relations with more than one person we find words like cheating and jealousy being less prevalent. In Deborah Anapol's book Polyamory for the Twenty First century she explores the different nuances of jealousy and how these can be resolved. this book is worth reading for this alone, yet is also interesting to see how people do relationship in different ways.
One thing that strikes me as true is simply that if you really love someone, why would you not be friends after the termination of your intimate relationship?

Why would you waste all that love?

Maybe it wasnt really love?

Maybe it was just convenience, chemicals of gratification and an array

of habits?

Further questions to ask include...
What are we doing with intimate relationship?

What are we doing with commitment?

What does commitment mean to us?

What do we want from committed intimacy?

We humans seem to do committed relationship quite badly. We seem to do polyamory even worse. What is the evolution of human relationship?

Sex at Dawn, how we mate and why we stray and what it means for modern relationship, by Christopher Ryan and Cacilda Jetha suggests we are evolved for fluid relational styles.

Sex at Dusk, lifting the shiny wrapping from Sex at Dawn, by Lynn Saxon shreds the pseudo science behind Sex at Dawn and reveals a completely different picture.

Neither book adeqately answers the question, what do we do with modern relationship?

How do we get our needs for safety, intimacy, ongoing relational sanctity and good sex all met through modern relationship?

The answer is in our co-evolutionary development and is yet to be defined.

Compersion
Compersion is the opposite to jealousy. Jealousy is arguably rooted in low esteem and a sense of loss. Compersion is rooted in high esteem and the recognition that nothing can be gained or lost, anywhere, ever.

Compersion places love for the other, the apparent other who is no other, above one's own feelings of possession, territory or control.

Can you enjoy the person you love being loved?
Can you enjoy their enjoyment or do you go into fear, jealousy and separation?
How real is your love if you experience un-love when they choose to explore with another?

Compersion celebrates other's successes, their win, their business deal, their qualification with authentic grace, clarity, compassion and presence.

Compersion is the opposite of schadenfreude.

Compersion is an extension of compassion, it is related to cultivating pleasure as well as authentically celebrating each other's joy and success. This kind of co-evolutionary behaviour shifts us out of the mindset of possession, ownership, revenge and the other dark and separate behaviours that otherwise arise when we feel rejected or challenged by shifts and changes in relational dynamics.

Lets begin to recognise and practice compersion as it draws us together into a web of love and connection rather than warfare and unlove.

Currency

currency is the eleventh key to conscious co-evolution

We humans have created systems of trade, built out of basic barter, since time immemorial. However, instead of simply trading one resource for another, such as furs for pig iron, or pottery for salt, we created a means of exchange we call money.
To make money work, an agreed value had to be placed on it so a fair exchange of so many deer hides or beaver furs for so many barrels of pig-iron could reasonably occur. After all the iron miner needed to know how much bread he could buy and the hide trader wanted to know how many deer or beaver he had to hunt before he could rest for the winter and make arrows.

Collectively agreed value on certain resources, such as gold, has been the means we have used to craft the basis of a system of trade. Gold has always been of special value, because it doesn't rust or tarnish and because it's reasonably rare, that particular element has been treasured. Yet gold itself has no intrinsic value any more than copper, rust or dust.

The whole Semitic, Arabic and Christian world have at various points described usury as a crime against God. Usury is where you lend someone ten pounds and demand eleven back, you take a percentage of profit on what you lent. But, we hear you ask, isn't that the foundation of capitalism?
Yes it is.
Capitalism is built on what was originally understood to be a crime against God and man. The criminal status of usury was lost under the Protestant church.
The Protestant church was originally poor, so to generate wealth it was consensually agreed that making money for God was a good thing. A mere couple of hundred years later the God bit was largely forgotten and just making money off money is a good thing! Along with the energy, drive, psychology and culture of the empire building activities rooted in the Norman crusades, capitalism was away, out of the starting blocks. So, today we have as a result, relentless consumption, profit

motive, gross national product and psychopathological leadership as key markers of a supposedly civilised society.

Money was then de-linked from the gold standard and we are left with currency. Currency is worthless in and of itself.
Currency is worth only what we believe it's worth, because currency does not exist.
Currency is a virtual commodity manufactured out of thin air by organisations such as The World Bank, The Federal Reserve, The International Monetary Fund, The Bank of England and other such private corporations. They simply decide how much currency a country is allowed and hey presto it exists.
When a government has a new flood of fabricated currency, they can then lend it to other commercial banks. These banks, also private corporations can then can lend out twenty times or so that amount; so that virtual commodity created out of thin air is magnified by the banks to create even more of this virtual commodity.
So, magic tricks aside, why does this matter and what has it to do with conscious co-evolution?

The conscious co-evolution, the social evolution of our species has focused very much on how to exchange and distribute resources and commodities. The system we have come up with so far was first barter, then money and now currency, and currency is simply what we trade our precious life-energy for. People across the globe are politically controlled by fear and debt. The flow of currency and the polarisation of this currency in the hands of the uber-wealthy elite affects us all in every aspect of our daily lives.
Given that our choices are relatively restricted on this planet without currency and given that people will often do anything for more currency, how do we co-create a world where the positive effects of equitable resource distribution outweigh the negative effects on human psychology, that the desire for more and more currency clearly can have.

This key point of conscious co-evolution takes us beyond the current orientation of commerce and the world economy as profit-centric, requiring endlessly increasing consumption and production of goods. Leaving resource distribution to a free market clearly does not ensure resources go where they are most needed, as we see with millions of human beings starving to death. Resource distribution under our current global economy goes to where people can most easily pay for them, as we see with fifty percent of the food reaching western countries being wasted.

Enlightened economics - economics as service

What would an enlightened global economics look and feel like if economics was rooted in service to humanity and not greed and grasping?

Would we be trading future commodities and resources, and in so doing push up prices on basic foodstuffs?

Would we be trading futures so that resource access for our children is likely to be compromised?

If not what would we be doing instead?

What actions can we take now to begin the transformations needed?

Would we have a super wealthy elite divided in almost every way from a hungry, landless and fearful poor?

What might work better for the benefit of all beings?

What might work better for the whole of humanity?

What might work better for this planet and its myriad species?

What is stopping us from co-creating this?

Will we still pretend we could possess, buy and sell strips of the planet's surface?

Will we still be destroying resources and paying no attention to the future of the planet and its populations of myriad species?

Or, will we be stewarding the land to promote and increase resources and develop mutual harmonious relationships with all the lifeform with which we share this planet?

How might we be doing this?

How will we begin doing this?

How might we craft our global culture in which contribution to the collective good is as natural as breathing?

How might we reward such a contribution to the collective, in whatever way it presents itself, with the means to a healthy and happy quality of life?

Would it be worth measuring the real wealth of nations in quality of life and gross national happiness, instead of movements of currency that are, in fact, fabricated?

In Bhutan they have four pillars to Gross National Happiness (GNH). They are

- The promotion of sustainable development
- Preservation and promotion of cultural values
- Conservation of the natural environment
- Establishment of good governance.

This is an example of what could be possible.
However we do it, real wealth is when the overall balance of financial, personal, collective, social and overarching environmental wellbeing are all taken into consideration.
Just having lots of money can make one very, very poor in every other aspect of development as a whole person.
Only a whole person can be really considered wealthy, others just have lots of stuff.
The question now arising is, how do we encourage our children to be whole, not partial people, shadows desperately chasing currency in endeavour to feel safe and happy in the relentless flow of impermanence?

As we have seen money is no longer connected to any real indicators of wealth anyway. Indicators such as resource, or happiness and wellbeing are divorced from money. Money was detached from the gold standard many years ago and now we have a currency that is essentially worthless, yet everyone pretends is valuable.

Why can't you and I fabricate money?

Why cant we then lend out twenty times that amount to our friends?

How have we agreed that only some people can fabricate currency and lend to their friends and the rest of us cant?

When such fabrication keeps some people in super-wealth and others in destitution how is this kind, reasonable, equitable, civilised, or evolved in any way?

What will our enlightened global economy look like?

It doesn't look like the one we have, that's for sure.
Arguably, real wealth begins with generosity and sharing. Grasping onto resource is simply one aspect of a pathological and scared ego. Let's begin to see 'super-wealth' as it is, largely pathological.
Anyone who feels they need vast quantities of money to be happy is probably a little out of touch with the realities of life. Maybe if such people practised yoga and meditation, found some authentic inner peace and contentment, then such pathology would be less prevalent.

Maybe if we all engaged in body, mind and heart training, found authentic realisation and appreciation for the flowing and impermanent nature of all phenomenal reality, then we could all relax a little more into the flow of life. Relaxed into the flow of life, with less gripping, less possessive territory making and other such aspects of a fear ridden life. Finding some authentic realisation of the non-dual, the one taste of emptiness-form, we could more easily co-create a culture, a community of wisdom and lovingness.

My belief is that only those free of grasping and attachment can wisely steward planetary resources for all, this should not be in the hands of pathological grasping beings. We simply steward and care for resources for future generations, there is realistically no possession.

At the risk of repeating, in my view it is better that resources are in the hands of evolved stewards, rather than egocentric insecure people who consistently seek identity, security, status, power and control through

the illusion of possession and dominance.
What are your feelings and thoughts about this?

How do we know what evolved stewards look and behave like?

Will they be somatically intelligent, emotionally intelligent, relationally intelligent, switched on individuals capable of working creatively in teams without pushing their own personal agenda?

Will they be people in service to humanity and the planet?
Probably.

How will we become such stewards?

We live on one planet with limits to its resources. Some of those limits are being rapidly approached. Some analysts believe we have even peaked with some resources, this means that from now on, some resources will get more and more expensive to access and use and will run out.
So, if we don't treat our resources as if they were precious and we just waste them on crass consumerist products, that's probably pretty stupid.
If we act as if our resources were limitless that's also probably pretty stupid.
Ok, but then our economic system is based on a philosophy of ever increasing production. Production and therefore resource use has to increase or the economic philosophy will be wrong. If it is wrong then everything that supports that philosophy is also questioned, thats about it. We have to rethink everything.

The current economic system and its operating philosophy is also supported by a legal system that states that the prime legal directive of any company is to return a dividend to its investors. In other words what comes first in global law and economics is profit. The planet, its people any myriad other species and the future of our children, the biosphere and all we value do not figure in the mathematics of profit.
Of course this sort of short term mathematics is ignorance. Not factoring in the longer term consequences of any action and seeing only the summation of profit in the very short term is facile. Right now the

packaging industry is making a profit, yet the ocean is being drowned in plastic waste. This plastic waste is having devastating effects on wildlife and ultimately human life. But it doesn't matter, profit is registered on the stock market. We could look at the low hanging fruit of fossil fuels, tobacco, sugar, armaments and pornography industries, all eminently profitable yet reaping catastrophe and huge expense for humanity in the longer term.

Shouldn't any legal, social and moral imperative clearly now state, planet and people first, future generations and quality of life first, whilst last of all comes profit.
Profit supports our values not drives them.

A truly enlightened economy would probably erase the very concept of 'profit' and possibly even money. When we have a systemic global governance, it will be all about systems and resource distribution not profit.

Since money is fabricated anyway, then the profits registered on todays market are as much an illusion as a desert mirage, a tedious trick of current market structures.
It's time for rethinking everything…
What creative new ways of stewarding and sharing resource will we come up with?

Which new ways will work best and how will we know?

Given we have this hugely inequitable greed/profit centred culture and that this disparity in wealth contributes to massive suffering on the planet, then four questions anyone interested in maximising human potential might ask are:
How will we design a fairer, more equitable system of resource allocation and distribution?

How are we are going to do build a fairer, enlightened and enlightening economy that actively develops human potential?

How will we ensure that each individual has the best prospects for sharing their creative human potential?

What will our enlightened, greed-free economy look and feel like?

This remains to be seen.
Bitcoin is vying for supremacy in new digital currencies and is now exchanged for national currencies. This exciting new arena of currency development will almost certainly be one of the new avenues of economic development.

Practitioners of conscious co-evolution are part of the process of crafting a world with a more enlightening economy, a world free of the motivations of greed and profit and driven by the motivations of service, contribution, sharing and really caring.
However we finally do it, such a new economy is a key to conscious co-evolution.

Carbon-Silicon Interface

the twelfth key to conscious co-evolution is the carbon-silicon interface

The carbon-silicon interface is here. Carbon and silicon intelligence are already synchronising. It's wise for us to pay attention and work as creatively, effectively and honestly as we can with this reality. We, as carbon based life-forms are creating silicon based artificial intelligence (AI), how we develop this interface is important.

Of course some of the primary research and much funding in the arena of this carbon-silicon interface is for the 'defence' industry. Terminator, Robocop and other sci-fi fantasises are no longer quite so fantastical.

We understand from our yogic practices of conscious co-evolution that no thing that appears separate really is separate, defined or independent.

We understand that the perceptual stories we create from the limitations of the senses fabricates this world of separation, substantiality, permanence and definition.

We understand the fractal, interdependent matrix as reality and all the separatist, materialist perceptual tales and views our minds tell us about reality are blown away, as the illusions they are. And, from the viewpoint of our nervous system and its senses, it's still all 'real'!

So, we cultivate the psycho-emotional tools to face and appreciate the pain and the bliss, the suffering and delight, the agony and the ecstasy of our neurological relationship with the flow of impermanence.

The current carbon-silicon interface we are familiar with is the keyboard and the screen. The interface we are familiar with from science fiction is a much deeper neurological interface, where the artificial intelligence of silicon and the organic intelligence of carbon based life-form (as homo-sapiens) merges in a range of cybernetic, cyborg and robotic possibilities that has until now seemed far-fetched. It's really not that far fetched any more.

A friend of mine ran a business working on voice recognition systems and these systems are getting so effective that credit card providers and countless other organisations now use highly responsive systems that mostly work very well. The vocal interface has been growing over the past ten years and has now landed as a part of our daily life.

Researchers at Zhejiang University in Huangzhou, China have developed a small quadcopter that is flown (fairly rudimentarily) by thought alone. This system converts brain-waves via an EEG machine through to a laptop with software that then controls the copter. The thought control of silicon devices in daily life is much closer than you might think.

The Paralympics in the UK was an amazing and profoundly powerful event. Humans with a whole variety of differing abilities pushed the edges of possibility and proved their power, determination, athletic capacity and human value despite formidable obstacles and difficulties. ***Can anyone who is not blind imagine participating in the blind long jump?***

We are at an edge of being able to provide neuro-prosthetics that will revolutionise the lives of people with physical disability.
The first silicon bridge has been used to help someone walk who had suffered a lumbar spinal break. Chair bound for seven years, this man was able to walk again. Yes it took considerable physiotherapy and yes there are ongoing complications, but that is nothing short of a miracle. Greg Clark at the University of Utah has produced a functional neuro-silicon connection for prosthetic hands so that a participant who lost both hands in an accident, a quarter of a century previously and has not touched anything for that long, feels a synthesised tactile sensation.

Artificial intelligence (AI), at the moment, is only good at what it's good at, sounds silly but its true. AI focuses only on specific tasks, such

as playing chess, finding web pages, flying drones and so on. AI currently lacks the capacity to act with generic intelligence. AI cannot yet complete the process of sensing its environment, gathering information, evaluating this information effectively, then modify it's knowledge base and it's perceptions and actions, whilst also act in a wide variety of modes based on this process. This process is what we do. This generic intelligence appears far off in the world of AI, but is it? Ben Goertzel of OpenCog an open-source AI project suggests this level of application is only ten to fifteen years away.
"Imagine an AI with sensors all over the planet, able to read thousands of web-pages and data sets at once and exchange data with other AI's via direct mind-to-mind file transfer" as Ben asks, because this is the way AI is heading.

A current theory of human individuated consciousness is called GWT. GWT stands for global workspace theory. Many autonomous brain regions harvest the sensory fields for information which only reaches what we call individuated consciousness, or what this theory calls the GWT when it is deemed important enough. Software that mimics the human global workspace is currently working with up to twenty thousand neurons, which offer one and a half million connections. The human brain comprises around one hundred and twenty billion neurons offering hundreds of trillions of synaptic connections. AI has a long way to go, but it's coming.

Lets look at the primitive way humans behave on this planet, from superstitious belief systems we give value to, relentless tribal battles of country against country and the simple fact that most people are happy reading tabloid newspapers full of mammaries, bigoted opinion, hearsay and gossip.
Not much productive use from that awesome bio-computer then?

The principle of the neuro-bot is simply that linking one simple twenty thousand-neuron unit to another and another, leads to a multiplicity of units where each unit is given responsibility for one simple function. Multiple units wired together gives a neuro-bot with several million neurons.
Maybe this is another way forward for AI?

I've mentioned the beginnings of neuro-linked prosthetics. We already wear computerised pacemakers and many other medical devices that support and measure life. Neuro-linked prosthetics connect directly from nerves into the mechanism of the mechanical appendage. So a replacement arm or leg can be controlled directly through mental control, rather like the Chinese quadcopter only a little more personal. Even more personal, if that's the word, we are beginning to grow body parts. The very first artificial tracheal transplant, where the artificial trachea was made of silicon surrounded with stem cells has been a success. Body parts will eventually be grown in labs from stem cells, no more need for donors. Body parts will be made that will allow those who were formerly disabled, super powers of physical capacity. The world as we know it is changing ferociously fast. The exponential drive of progress is only getting faster. We can only glimpse and science-fantasize about how life will be in fifty years let alone five hundred, given we deal with climate change and manage the manifold problems of accelerating global temperatures.

As we build on adaptive signal processing, neuro-silicon interfaces, computerised reasoning, artificial creativity through modular synergy, the use of systems modelling and real computerised learning then we know that the carbon-silicon interface is not far away, it's already here.

We are also on the verge of the next level of supercomputer too, this is also on its way. A whole range of possible mechanisms for its structure are being tested, from chlorophyll from plants through to mono-molecular sheets of carbon interlaced with silicon, graphene or other compounds. The quantum computer is on its way. One of the current limitations of computing is the cooling of the chips. When the quantum computer finally lands we may be using hand held, or even implanted computers that have the capacity of modern super-computers, like those possessed by organisations such as NASA or Google. Quantum computers will have speeds of operation that will transcend anything we can currently conceive. Such computers will be used in every arena of exploration and life from personal to medical and scientific inquiry and we may even have direct neural access to all the information stored on the web. Now that is scary!

The progress of touch screen computing has been limited, to a degree, by the scarcity of the minerals required to create the screens, and hampered by the strategic politics of who controls these resources. However, new substances and new designs are constantly being made available. One product uses micro-tubules derived from wood waste. From these micro-tubules touch screens, 'metallic' vehicle parts and 'plastic' can all be made. This nano-crystalline cellulose, which is also bio-degradable appears to be totally harmless. We also have the possibility of making silicon based nano-tubules from sand that can be used in the semiconductor industry. Yet, whether touch screens will become a historic footnote remains to be seen. If direct neural-silicon interfaces become common the human mind, as I said could be directly 'wire-lessed up' to the world-wide-web. We will be the world-wide-web, with all its vast flows of information, spam and carbon based citta chatter (that's a yoga joke for those who understand Sanskrit terms for aspects of mind) as well as any dark web, the shadow internet.

As for energy production we have phenomenal capacities becoming available through our scientific endeavour. Bio-fuels leader Jonathan Trent is showing the world how to grow as much carbon-neutral fuel as we need. We also have all we need to make enough electricity through solar concentrating mirrors for current planetary energy usage, that's before we even look to wind-power, geo-thermal, biomass generators, wave power or any other means.
The remaining question is why are we still drilling for oil and gas when they are so passé?

Hybrid airplanes have been designed and could be put into production, especially with the new micro-tubule nano-technology, graphene, kevlar or other such super substances that can produce lightweight and super-strong fuselages. We could be running this beautiful planet on carbon-neutral energy sources within twenty years - with the right investment and the political will. Yes, we really could!

Consumer virtual-reality devices are here. Oculus Rift and HTC Vive are now here for people to have powerful embodiment experiences as an avatar. It's possible that they will feel rather insignificant and disembodied in their own body after such an immersion in hyper-reality. People using these devices may get used to carrying out acts of gratuitous violence or pornographic acts as an avatar. Given their brains won't be able to elicit the difference between virtual silicon and 'real' carbon based realities, they may behave differently after their virtual immersion. If their avatar is a different morphology, their psychological attributes may also be changed from those that their carbon based identities invite. These are some of the serious issues in the face of hyper reality that are largely being bypassed in the drive for this new and profitable adventure.

Squabbling power hungry nations, competing religions of humanity and organisations focused solely on profit are still busy wrapping themselves in vested beliefs, mediaeval mindsets and self-interested behaviour oriented around personal wealth aggrandisement and accumulation of power as dominance. All this is still considered as 'the way' of doing business on this beautiful planet, we have a long way to go before we can consider ourselves civilised. We have a lot of groundwork to do simply to to utilise all the amazing technology available to us with which we can create a sustainable future. We have much work to do to transform and limit the damaging practices of the present, and co-create a systemically wise future that is worth living.

Of course the future is always different to our imaginings and the current explorations around graphene point to a carbon-silicon-graphene interface of very interesting potential.
I don't know what will happen, do you?

Whether we like it or not though, the carbon-silicon interface and all it's scary, exciting and promising possibilities is not going away.
Here lies a choice between paying attention to and co-creating the future from the integrity of our vision, or hiding our heads under our meditation cushions and wishing for a return to some golden age.
The carbon-silicon interface is not going away. Either we ignore it or we work with it. Let's work consciously with this powerful leading edge of our co-evolution.

Commensals and symbionts

the thirteenth key to conscious co-evolution is our microbiome, the micro-organisms that our life depends on

We are completely dependent on our microbial load, our microbiome for our life.

Some theories suggest that our biological make up is a symbiont. We are a mix of different life forms. Our mitochondria, the organelles in our cells that make all our energy may well have originated as a separate lifeform that was incorporated into our cellular makeup. Some theorists even go so far as to say that the nuclei in our cells were a separate lifeform that was incorporated.

So, as you read this, what you think of as your body may well be a symbiont of three ancient lifeforms including perhaps an ancient virus and a bacterium, we don't really know but it brings a little humility to the arrogance of the human species.

Our body has ten times more microbial cells than 'human' cells. The organisms in our guts assist our digestion. Not only that but when they get imbalanced we can get obesity issues, arthritic, depressed, anxious, rheumatic, asthmatic, cardiovascular disorders and other life threatening conditions. Our microbes may also be involved in muscular sclerosis, autoimmune conditions and potentially even autism.

The microbes on our skin help us regulate temperature and sustain immunity. Microbes in the Yoni (vagina) facilitate health and wellbeing for the mother and the baby. As a baby is born it is coated in these microbes which facilitate good immune function and overall health in the newborn. When this transfer does not occur, through non-vaginal birth for example, babies are more susceptible to respiratory allergies, digestive problems and many other conditions where compromised immunity is involved.

A powerful research backed suggestion is that we only find other

people attractive as intimate partners, when our gut bacteria are compatible. If someones microbiome is incompatible with ours we won't find them attractive. We will find their smell disturbing. This allies with pheromonal attraction, so we find someone's smell attractice when our bloods major histocompatability complex's (MHC) dovetail to offer any potential progeny effective immune function.
So is it our microbes in conjunction with our MHC that decide our intimate partners for us?

The study of the health implications of an imbalanced microbiome is just beginning to be studied. We know very little at the moment as to what balances of organisms work best for different individuals. We do know they are crucial to our health and to our continued survival.
So, when people or products promise to kill 99% of all known germs, it is best to stay away and keep your populations of healthy micro-organisms vibrant and strong.
Babies spending time in a stable in their first few hours (Jesu got it right), and children growing up with a dog in the house are much less likely to develop asthma, why?
It is most possibly to do with micro-organisms.

Some people suggest that water should be de-chlorinated before drinking it, as drinking chlorinated water might harm your gut flora and fauna.
Some people recommend consuming keffir, kombucha, kim-chee and other fermented and microbially relevant products in an endeavour to build better strength, wellbeing and immunity. It is certainly not good to be too squeaky clean, your microbiome wont be happy.

There is now an explosion of neutriceuticals based on microbial theory of wellbeing being commercially exploited. We really know way too little to be selling any such product at the moment. Along with this people are offering faecal transplants, where you eat someone elses excrement as a way of imbibing their microbes. Soem people report tragic side effects from e-coli infection to obesity and others report amazing health transformation from both faecal transplants and neutriceuticals. The microbial health market is unregulated and we just don't have enough information to know what is the best course of action with regard to microbiual oriented treatments.

My belief is that if we eat realtively unprocessed foods with minimal sugar we grow good microbes. I also believe it is good to exercise and move, breathe well, think well, meditate well, play well and have time in nature. In my experience, this kind of healthy lifestyle breeds good mibcrobes inside and out.

In terms of empirical evidence, we just don't know enough about this important topic at the moment, we just know that it is very important. This will change.
Watch this space and be grateful for all the invisible little beasts that keep you alive and kicking.

One thing you can be sure of, as we co-evolve, our microbiome will be co-evolving with us. Another thing you can be sure of, we will have to pay attention to our commensals and symbionts and garden them well.

Comedy

the fourteenth key to conscious co-evolution is comedy

Comedy is rooted in the capacity to juxtapose opposites in unexpected ways, and in ways of presenting paradox in unexpected yet accessible form. Comedy is a means of easing fear and playing with the edges of consensual reality.
Comedy is totally awesome.

Comedy has been shown to help people who are suffering from depression and to speed healing rates for other illnesses, hence Dr Patch Adams work with accelerating healing through laughter. The funny thing about comedy is that we all find different things funny, some of us laugh at slapstick and others at quite dark humour.
However we do it, comedy works.

Comedy works to bring politicians and religious leaders down to size, it resolves the tendency to turn people into demigods. Comedy is, amongst many other things the irreverent antidote to deification.

Higher primates laugh. They laugh to ease social distress and uncertainty, it's a means of resolving social tension. We primates laugh as a way of dispelling fear. Laughter and tears are so closely related, as we know that the edges between fear and laughter can be crossed so easily. Dolphins also appear to laugh, they certainly play and have large enough brains to get the joke of appearing to be separate things.

We human beings take ourselves so seriously, and yet when we resolve our illusion of separateness it is humour that arises as a key quality of awakened mind. A Yogi really is known by their laugh!

When a person no longer takes the universe personally, when the dualities of existence and impermanence no longer worry such a character, then laughter is the natural response. I was fortunate to spend a short time with some Vietnamese monks who spoke little or no English and I little French. The ninety-four year old monk and the diminutive eighty-year old communicated through resonance and ebullient and infectious laughter.

When our clever minds reach the point where we finally realise that the universe is so much more complex and beautiful than any concept we can throw at it, when we realise that our stunning bio-computers that work in dualistic conceptual patterning cannot really grasp the vastness and intricacy of the cosmos and whatever is beyond, only then, as we drop out of conceptual mind, can we can begin to see and appreciate the sane responses of total awe, sublime bio-philia and heartfelt laughter.

Yes, comedy is a co-evolutionary act.

So, the twelfth evolutionary art is having a laugh! Which reminds me, did you hear the one about the Buddha selling hot dogs?

Celebration and Ceremony

the fifteenth key to conscious co-evolution is celebration and ceremony

These are two of the important ways we come together to celebrate shared meaning, generate deeper community and explore collective meaning making.

Some of us still come together to celebrate natural transitions and cycles. I create ceremony at new moons and full moons. New moons appear to fill brains more with acetylcholine, the neurotransmitter of creative endeavour. Full moons appear to fill brains more with dopamine, the neurotransmitter of anticipation, celebration and completion.

Historically we have always celebrated solar cycles of solstices and equinoxes as well as the points between these. The bringing together of community in shared meaning has always been a powerful facet of being human.

Nowadays we use new year celebrations, which are artificial, socially constructed events but nonetheless potentially powerful. We use football matches and sporting events, many still use church meetings or religious gatherings as well as religious festivals.

The celebration of birth, menstruation, motherhood, fatherhood and many other life transitions is how we do what we do to generate the experience of being family, community and humanity.

Ceremony is the collective creation or celebration of shared meanings. We have done this for as long as we have been human. The forms change, the meanings we put behind things change but we keep doing it.
Why?

Because it works, it joins us, it helps us feel more connected, more cohesive, more understood, more a part of something bigger than us and more powerful. We can also suspend analysis and meaning making, because all that is done for us in the collective field of ceremony.

Some traditions have used drum, dance and mind altering 'medicines' to take their participants into theta brain wave states. Obviously we have to respect the law of the land wherever we work, however every culture uses exogenous substances to initiate brain states that are perceived as useful or functional for that community, whether caffeine or alcohol, sugar or television or more expansive and possibly helpful substances.
The question is...
Are they actually helpful for generating prosocial behaviour, intense learning states, cultural healing or enhanced community or not?

Communal theta state is an intense socialised learning state that allows the reframing and repositioning of perceived social ills and the resolution and healing of these.
Ceremony has been used to enter brain wave states together where the need fro meaning making and analysis is temporarily suspended.

When we suspend these functions of analysis and meaning making our powers of belief are more easily activated activated. Rationality can support belief, but needs to be suspended for belief to be powerful.

Having an overarching meta-narrative and collectively agreed view on the nature of things helps us be powerful belief-beings. As a belief-being, or a belief-artist we can heal, transcend obstacles and access aspects of ourselves that we cannot do through rationality. Ideally the two sisters of belief and rationality support each other, if they do we can truly begin to access our potential as a human being.

Our belief is powerful, we are placebo, we activate healing and the capacity to manifest our dreams (through appropriate action) when we believe sufficiently in a principle, purpose , process or meta-narrative.

I find the space I access inside myself in ceremonial circles is incomparable to any thing I can create alone. I celebrate my need for others and seek new ways of welcoming ceremony into the twenty-second century and beyond.

Part of being human is collective celebration and ceremony. Lets build celebration and ceremony in conscious co-evolution with each other to facilitate unicity within the species and with our systemic source, this amazing planet.

Conflict Resolution

the sixteenth key to conscious co-evolution is conflict resolution

In human relational events, conflicts happen.
When conflicts happen how do we choose to mediate and resolve them?

Human beings have carried out acts of war for the extent of human history, except maybe some early cultures such as Mohenjo Daro. Scholars suspect the complete lack of weapons and war imagery may inidcate a peaceful culture. Human beings have also lived in peace and sought peaceful solutions to conflict.
With the advent of modern technological warfare, we can see just how destructive warfare is, of resource, civilisation and the environment.

In many contemporary schools, conflicts are mediated and resolution sought through clear processes of considered action. When bullying and aggression occur the situation is brought to conflict resolution and slowly resolved. Fundamentally, the recognition exists that someone who sources their feel-good factor and esteem by bullying others is unhappy inside.

Meanwhile, some governments still go to war to 'resolve' issues, leading to the death or disablement of thousands of (often innocent) individuals in horrific circumstances. Ironically, and consequentially this manifests many more issues for the survivors of such atrocities.
How are we going to co-create a planet where conflict resolution is carried out with clear process and intelligence, not with aggression, mindless brutality and horrific weaponry?

Conflict happens, let's accept it, it's totally natural. Waves crash onto rocks wearing the rocks away or smashing them into oblivion. The sun evaporates pools of water and rain dissolves buildings. Antelope eat grass and tigers eat antelopes. Everywhere we look there's conflict, at least if we look honestly. Yet if we look everywhere then we also find the resolution of conflict.

In human society conflict can be considered to be part of its evolution and development. To date, much conflict still escalates into full-blown warfare.
The opportunity for creatively harnessing the energy underlying conflict as a developmental tool is either lost, or left to the unconscious vicissitudes and flows of space-time.

Conflict always provides creative and growth opportunities and therefore can be seen as an event that is not inherently negative. It is an arising of energy that can be a powerful force for change if it can be harnessed effectively and worked with to the end of peace-building. This is the art of conflict management.

Conflict in human society is becoming increasingly expensive and a waste of human and other resources. Despite the fact that, historically, war has boosted many failing economies it is a complete waste of human and ecological resource.

For sure, the defence industries initiate a lot of awesome scientific research. The funding could still be there, it doesn't have to be routed through the armaments industry. Some of the current research on robots via the emerging carbon-silicon interface is aimed at creating super robotic warriors.

Sadly, it seems that what some of us humans are doing at our current level of development is funding, researching and creating even more effective death machines. To grow out of this mindset and behaviour is an evolutionary project that requires awareness, clear choice, loving dedication and real commitment.

The emerging science of conflict management is a part of this growth. The simple recognition that conflict can be hugely destructive and expensive is at long last making this psychological study viable and worthwhile.

The inner work of yoga, tantra, meditation and mindfulness offers key tools for the safe handling of conflict starting with central nervous

system management, somatic exploration and awareness of internal dynamics and motivations, as well as ultimately making the self-construct conscious and no longer the driver of our behaviour.
When we no longer grip onto egocentric, ethnocentric and religiocentric beliefs, we can live more peacefully.

The reduction and management of conflict evidenced in other species certainly has evolutionary value. There is often a lot of postruing in wild animals and realtively little actual fighting.

The emerging science of conflict management probably occupies a similar role for us. Either we use conflict creatively through conflict management skills or we create such complex conditions for our own and other species that we head inexorably to extinction.

The Five Limbs of an Integral Conflict Resolution System (ICRS)

- Culturally promoted creation of personal skills of inner awareness and conflict resolution

- Managing the arising energy of conflict, using it creatively whilst pre venting the escalation of conflict into all out war

- Facilitating the rapid end of escalated social conflict or warfare

- Post conflict peace-building

- Co-creating a culture that self-regulates for creative conflict manage ment and active peace-building

I would love to see this 'conscious co-evolution theory' of conflict resolution, or an even better one, in place as a cultural norm.
Understanding the art of communication as in the previous chapter is key to this development.

As it arises, conflict is usually related to a struggle for autonomy, power or to secure resources for groups or individuals. Co-creating a culture where the 'common ground' is an embedded cultural construct would craft a social environment required to facilitate the above pentagon of conflict resolution skills as a cultural norm.

One of my sons was at a school in the UK where a degree of conflict resolution using mediation was in place, with relative effect and making a big difference on playground bullying. Such strategies can really work. At the same time the 'adults' in western governments were belligerently going to war on what now transpire to be trumped up pretences, and we're doing it again!
What sort of example is this?

What happened to the political leaders (war criminals in need of psychological help) who created this conflict?

How was this allowed to happen?

Contextual Frames of an ICRS

Five further strategies in conflict resolution and peace-building that give a contextual frame to the whole process of the ICRS are: -

- Consistently remembering and celebrating our common ground.

In conscious co-evolution we do this daily through touching into awareness, breath, heartbeat and our experience of centre of gravity and vertical central line. As we start and finish practice we know this is true of all beings. It is a daily practice of common ground.

- Negotiation. Dialogue between involved parties. Involved parties have to believe they get more from dialogue than engaging in escalating conflict.

- Compromise. Where involved parties are willing to reduce some part of their demands on resources or others in concern for the common good.

- Mediation. Conflict resolution facilitated by a third party who seeks to open and improve dialogue and lead towards any necessary com promise and peace-building. This is a real opportunity for creative use of the energy of conflict to deepen awareness for all and craft

social possibilities of deeper mutual engagement and understanding.
- Cooperation, where the triad of Concern for self, Concern for others and Concern for the common good are held so effectively in balance that conflict management and resolution becomes an art.

- The strategies of avoidance where parties just hope it will all go away rarely work.

- Strategies of yielding to oppressive forces rarely work long- term.

- Strategies of competition, seeking to win, rarely work out for the greatest common good where win-win-win is needed.

- Conciliation can work, this is where one seeks to regulate conflict through demand accountancy - I'll give up this demand if you give up that one...

The art of ICRS is essential in our contemporary world. It is an art form and a science, one we would do well to embed within our global culture.

The internalisation practices of awareness from conscious co-evolution are the first limb of this art of ICRS.

Many people look back into the past to some golden age or another, the Satya Yuga, the land of Ogyen, Atlantis, or whatever it may be for them. Personally I am relatively disinterested in such speculative stories and romantic notions, however delightful. I am however, deeply interested in the golden age we are co-creating, co-evolving. My questions is...
What are we crafting in this moment?

This moment is the co-evolution of the golden age, the age of now, and in this moment and from this moment the age yet to come.
It is conscious co-evolution and the broad awareness this demands that leads us forward into this moment and all moments. This moment is the open-hearted realisation of complete indivisibility and inseparability that leads us into the new golden age, the new earth of this moment and all moments.

In conscious co-evolution we neither look back in regret or romantic whimsy, nor do we look forward in fear.
We simply look around in appreciative, vast awareness and act wisely and lovingly from this place and then, in this moment, exists the golden age.

Slowly we will craft a world where all beings know themselves as indivisible from each other and will treat each other with simple kindness, respect, appreciation, interest and even love.

Conflict resolution, not conflict is the promise of conscious co-evolution. This is the work of conscious co-evolution.

Contentment

the seventeenth key to conscious co-evolution is contentment

In a consumption oriented culture contentment is a rarity. Contentment is a state of being at peace with the cosmos, nothing needs to be any different, right now, to make anything any better. It's all good. Contentment is a sublime acceptance or all arising and flowing phenomena including that of one's own body-mind.

Contentment is considered to be a spiritual state that is certainly taught in yogic systems as a precursor to yogic practice and as an outcome of yogic practice. It is an understanding that in the universe, everything that could happen is happening and it is the capacity to relax into this flow.

Relaxing into the flow, as flow and being fully present as this is the root of powerful change. It is from the base of neurological contentment that opportunity and leverage can be clearly seen and acted on effortlessly.
There is plenty of empirical evidence that people with over a certain amount of wealth are not happier than those with less.
Money does not necessarily give contentment of happiness.

Contentment is not passive acceptance or resignation.
Contentment is like a fish swimming downstream, moving within the flow and current. Passive acceptance or resignation is like a dead fish, resigned to being battered against rocks, there is no skill of being with the flow in a healthy way.

Contentment is not the opposite of pro-social change, contentment is part of the means for pro-social change. Contentment is also the outcome of pro-social change.

When the clear need arises then action for pro-social change is taken through individual or concerted collective action with the full feeling of contentment of the necessity for this engagement.

Contentment is a state of being that understands and computes seamlessness and therefore allows appropriate flow in any and every direction.
Let's practice this kind of contentment.

Conservation of diversity

the eighteenth key to conscious co-evolution is conservation of diversity

We are the breath of the trees, hippy though that sounds, we cannot separate ourselves from the vegetation of planet earth, nor can we find ourselves separate from the wind or the earth which constitutes our flesh or the raina nd rivers which make up our blood.

When the wolves were returned to Yellowstone Park the ecology changed because deer were no longer able to graze and denude the landscape at will. As the plant diversity regrew so did a host of other creatures.

If a tiny shrimp, the crill in the ocean are challenged by changing oceanic temperature or increased carbon dioxide in the water (they can't make their shells in more acidic water) then all the life of the oceans are at stake.
We live in and are part of a web of interconnection.
The stability of the web is dependent on its biodiversity, upon their existing a multitude of inter-dependent life form.

As we increase our population, now upward of seven billion and increase our agricultural expansion to feed the wealthier end of this population, we change the landscape and reduce biodiversity.
We cut down forests, drain swamps and marshes, kill predators, eradicate weeds (plants growing where we don't want them to grow), and kill pests (animals living where we don't want them to live) to enable us to grow more food.
A full half of this food is wasted in wealthier countries.
A lot of this production is also nutritionally-light belly filler, or to feed animals raised in inhumane conditions to make cheap protein.

We control water courses and change the way floodplains work to support life. We build massive dams and change the way rivers work to

support life.
Our dams also put vast pressure on the crust of the earth and some scientists suggest they contribute to earthquakes.
Our burning of fossil fuels has been evidenced by ninety percent of peer reviewed, methodologically sound empirical scientific studies to be the biggest factor in the changing climatic conditions we face on planet earth. The studies that say otherwise are often funded by oil companies.

Sadly we live in such an age of misinformation that even crucial truth is being hidden under a morass of 'alternative truth' promoted by vested interests.

Our consumption focused activity and the industries and political systems that support it are putting thousands of species at risk. Human beings are carrying out the largest and fastest mass extinction, possibly in the history of this planet.

Even now, in Japan, a robotic bee has been invented so that we can forget about caring for those darned critters upon which our life depends.
Lets forget the bees yes?

No, let's not.
We tolerate other life form if we can eat it, if it can be a pet, if it doesn't affect us or get in our way or if we clearly need it to survive.
Otherwise why bother, let them die, they're no use to us, are they?

Heck lets tolerate trees shall we?

No regard for the fact that trees produce our breath. No regard for the fascinating web of sentience and inter-plant communication that goes on in a forest. No regard for the vast community of creatures that the forest supports. Hey, we're inventing super-chlorophyll from bacteria so we can create genetically modified super plants. That way we can grow super crops and feed ourselves. Maybe we can grow super trees in monocultures to produce oxygen and timber and let those forests die. Bang goes the Amazon forest.
We need the space to grow soya beans so we can feed cattle and eat more burgers anyway. Let the Amazon die. Let the Indonesian forests

die, we need more palm oil for more cheap baked goods.
Who cares about forests?

Sarcasm aside, that's the attitude we as a species are evidencing or we would be collectively acting to care for the forests, the oceans, the polar ice caps and all the ecological niches and their denizens. As individuals we would be insisting on it and not voting in ecologically naive and culpable leaders.

If we weren't evidencing such pathologically vast ignorance, ignorant indifference, we would be acting collectively to insist on powerful changes.

We cannot do it alone, we have to work collectively, globally in concerted action to do something about this situation.
Yes, the dark web of corporate power and money and the military that goes with them will probably be turned against those who make any stand for this, our home and its life form.

The current leaders of our planet appear to be ecologically insane, why do we allow them to be in power, because they are good at convincing us that we can keep doing business as usual?

We have leaders of several nations now who don't believe in climate science, like it were something to believe in or not?

Science is not a liberal conspiracy, it is a method of investigating what is true and real. These leaders and their financial supporters in the fossil fuel industry and other industries focused on mass consumption are palpably engaged in ecocide.

By neglect, omission and commission they are engaged in a programme to destroy lifeform on this, our planet, on a scale that is genocidal beyond our reckoning.
Why do we allow it?

Why have we voted them in?

Good questions.

Maybe we are more concerned with our comfort, our centrally heated or air conditioned homes, what's on TV and on our plates than we are concerned about a habitable planet for our children and our children's children?

Somebody had to name Hitler's crimes, what happened to the Native Americans, the Aboriginal Australians and other First Nation peoples as genocide.
Somebody has to name the neglect, omissions and actions of the political and corporate elite insistent on promoting consumption and fossil fuel usage as ecocide, and as mass genocide, simply because it is.

If we are to make this planet habitable for our children and our children children we have to suspend the mythology that we are separate from nature, somehow above it, and learn to live as part of it.

We have to learn to be stewards and care for the planet, for its myriad lifeforms, its biodiversity and put our consumption and profit underneath care and concern for our home, this beautiful planet. This is the focus and vision of conscious co-evolution.

Collective Decision Making

the nineteenth key to conscious co-evolution is collective decision making

Once upon a time, all decisions were made by the noblesse oblige. Before that they were made in a whole variety of ways in agrarian communities, city states and tribal and hunter gatherer groups.

The noblesse oblige were, and still are, the pathological few who believed they had the 'divine right' to rule over those whose destiny it was to be a lower order of humanity, the serfs. These overlords were in clear allegiance with religious leaders, and anybody who disagreed with their dictates was brutally punished.

Since then we have evolved to a slightly more democratic model of some accountability where some of the population (about sixty percent of the electorate turn out for elections in the U.S and the U.K.) vote for one of two or more 'agenda-driven' groups of people, who are supposed to represent the electorates viewpoints and desires. This means thirty percent of the electorate get to be the 'will of the people'.

The reality is still that the groups who can vie for power are funded by vast quantities of money. They have to be backed by big money or they would not be able to stand. Some of this money is so hidden it is called dark money, money that is spent on persuasion engineering to get 'the will of the people' to be what the wealthy elite (the owners of the dark money) want it to be.

The reality is that a pseudo-accountability exists, which is opaque at times, as we keep seeing with the corruption evident in politicians, globally. The relentless appearance of politicians lining their own pockets as they kowtow to big business is becoming rather jaded for the ordinary man and woman struggling to pay the rent or mortgage and feed and educate their children.

The reality appears to be a charade, with the only power the electorate having is to put a mark on a piece of paper every few years or so and then stand in the streets and protest if they don't like what their elected 'representatives' are doing. Their 'elected representatives' may then turn the full brutality of the forces of law and order on them for their vocal inquiry and prohibit such public inquiry into the issues being explored.

To date, this is how we have collectively chosen to make decisions. And even this is rare! Across most of the world such liberty is still a long way off. Many people still live in regimes where religious dictators, secular dictators, power groups or other forms of dictatorial control still dominate political process.
Is this really the best we can do as an intelligent, informed species?

In some contemporary groups of humans seeking an evolutionary decision-making process the focus is on consensus.
Consensus is where issues are discussed over time and the whole group come to an agreement about the best way forward. This is a fantastic idea and certainly has more collective involvement than the divine right, dictatorial or democratic models of decision-making.
One aspect of consensus that can become problematic is the issue of gripping onto points of view. If one person in the group is stubbornly insistent on their viewpoint or agenda and can hang on interminably then the whole process can be undermined. In contrast to those who dominate groups, are those who rest relatively uninvolved, both strategies sabotage the authenticity of consensus.

One means to resolve this problem is to co-create a culture of participation and consensus where a feeling of common ground is sought. We always have common ground. We all need food, shelter, water and good relationships within and outside our community. When we recognise this common ground is what we are all seeking, then we can potentially arrive at a decision where the result will serve the greater good. This approach transcends the preoccupation with merely advancing our personal opinions, viewpoints and agenda.
A culture of participation is facilitated when people are valued for their contribution, and each contribution is seen as a gift to the group, a gift

that will assist the synergy of problem solving.
There is evidence that in decision-circles the collective intelligence of the group comes into play.

Collective intelligence is a synergy where solutions to problems are more easily and more fully found. The positive solution focused culture of seeking common ground and mutual participation has to be present for this to work effectively. This balances the more competitive and challenging energies we humans do so well.

I was involved in a test run for another model of community decision making which worked well. Like any model it has its weaknesses too, and areas that could do well with being ironed out. See if you can spot these weaknesses.
Decisions fall into different levels of gravity. There are always smaller, less influential decisions and larger, more complex issues to sort out in any community. Having five (plus or minus two) different levels of decision complexity is one approach. For example, we might have simpler level-one decisions, such as how do we decide who does the washing up, shopping or cooking? A level-four decision has much greater complexity, such as which new property do we buy and why? A different consensus time-frame is attributed to each level of decision. This means that with the culture of consensus in place the aim for the group was to find a solution to the problem within that time frame. The time frame was expansive enough to allow deep discussion of all the issues involved and included several sittings to explore all the issues.
Another aspect of this puzzle was to seek and share as much information as possible allowing informed, evidence based, decision making. The time-frame concept, consensus culture, information rich process and seeking common ground encourage finding decisions that work for the whole community.
If the time frame was transcended without consensus being reached then the decision process devolved to the democratic model and a majority vote was taken and followed.
What are some of the issues with this process?

Who decides which issue fits into which decision level?
Second, if vested groups of interest still choose to they can extend the discussion to go beyond the consensus frame and push to get a majori-

ty vote that they feel they can win.
Would it work at a city, national or international level?

Probably not at the moment, but maybe.
As a base for effective decision making we have to look at how we grow our culture, we have to work with culture creation as the pre-requisite for any enlightened decision-making process.

Can you come up with better models?

Share them please.
Conscious co-evolution is about co-creating an awakened planet. Conscious co-evolution practitioners choose to look at these areas of human process so we can bring the light of love, wisdom and responsible freedom to all our relational experiences.

We learn to love by being mutually involved. Learning to love is what we're all doing. When we consciously recognise this and are willing to let our family, friends and community help us, it gets a whole lot easier.

Conscious Culture Creation

the twentieth key is awareness and action in pro-social culture creation

Firstly, it's good to recognise that we continuously co-create culture. We are a culture creating species.
Culture is the collective framework in which we help incubate and mature our future generations. Usually, culture is co-created unconsciously based on historical precedent and cultural mythology.

This chapter, and maybe the whole book, is about the co-creation of a culture that is rooted in pragmatic, systemic, ethical and integral values.

These values are not being presented as some form of ultimate truth but simply as a method of understanding. Method yields a specific outcome. The outcome of method I am interested in is one whereby human beings know themselves as an integral part of the matrix of inseparability.
When this outcome occurs the secondary outcomes are in human behaviour to each other.

This has been espoused throughout this book with reference to yogic tradition, philosophy, practice and contemporary psychology and neuroscience. The cultural behaviour of realised practitioners of Conscious co-evolution is ideally kind, aware and promotes mutual freedom.

Part of the brain that give us our sense of separateness include the posterior parietal and the insula. If these parts of the brain are damaged then people we cannot function effectively.
In conscious co-evolution we are seeking to transcend the function of this part of the cortex through cognitive recognition, affective connection and kinaesthetic realisation as well as gradually resetting the HPAA, and transforming brain function.
As the left pre-frontal cortex becomes more prominent then it has the capacity to generate non-contextual joy and greater executive control

so can functionally disinhibit the posterior parietal. As we also learn to generate theta states and gamma synergy in the brain then healing of past trauma and its resultant neuroses can occur as we move into post-traumatic growth.

It is also possible that the arising joy, that is the fruit of meditative practice can be communicated as a neurological state throughout the brain.

This section may well prove to be complete 'fruitloopery' to use the term from New Scientist for unadulterated pseudo-science.

It's a working theory I'm running with in the absence of supportive empirical research.

We do however know that long term meditators have greater left pre-frontal activity and that this leads to greater and more prolonged states of non-contextual joy.

We do know that long term meditators report greater gamma synergy and that this brainwave pattern may be connected to uniform, congruent brain functionality.

It is theorised that entering theta brainwave states may facilitate greater learning states and healing.

We do know that through chanting and drumming we can more easily enter theta states.

Ken Wilber evidences entering various brain wave states at will on YouTube, he is a meditator.

Conscious co-evolution amongst many other aspects of achieving optimal function is intended to teach us to manage and master our own central nervous systems including wilfully entering lucid dreams states and all the positive consequences of that.

So, whilst this is in its fullness pure speculation, there is increasing support offered as to the effects of meditative practice.

As an aside, one of the interesting results of the Shamatha Project, a three month research project from 2010-11 on meditators, was that the meditators telomeres appeared to grow. Telomeres define cell longevity and cell death. They have been considered only to reduce with every cell replication. Now we know that some contexts such as meditation allow cell telomeres to grow, which potentially increases longevity. Another piece of research has shown that meditators experience time as passing slower. So this might mean that mediators have potentially increased longevity, a slower passage of time and more joy.

In William Broads book, The Science of Yoga he points out research that suggests that yoga practice makes people feel sexier and have a more satisfying sex life. So we have longer life, more time, greater joy, feeling sexier and more satisfaction. Sounds good to me, I'll have some of that please!

Our culture is relatively recently post-feudal. In the UK we still have feudal overlords and clergy in government, and a feudal monarchy as head of state. We still have an active class culture rooted in noblesse oblige and the right to rule of the feudal overlords, these are still the ruling class. Feudal monarchs had to be pathological simply to survive and breed. They had to be ready to torture, impale, behead, crucify, slaughter, commit genocide or whatever was perceived necessary to sustain their lineage, their nation, their control and their wealth.

In sublimated form, these qualities have permeated to the political business world. Psychological testing indicates that we still tend to unconsciously (or consciously) select for these qualities amongst business leaders and politicians. Many people still revere such feudal characteristics as representative of greatness.
I, however, don't. I value somatic intelligence, emotional literacy and intelligence, systemic intelligence, relational intelligence and integral intelligence far above the feudal values that society currently promotes.

I believe it is necessary to completely rethink culture and find new ways to grow and build culture that are free of the unhealthy distortions of the past.
Would any sane culture promote psychopathology in their children's lives if they knew it was possible to resolve and eliminate it?

No.
Would any sane culture continue practices into the future that destroyed the environment and potentially led to a mass extinction on this planet?

No.
So, we have to rethink and co-create conscious culture. There is not really much alternative.
Culture is always based on what came before.

Can we filter the baby from the bathwater though and eliminate all the destructive aspects of our past history?

Culture, being based on what came before, is rife with elements of 'it was always done like that so it has to continue'...
Does it though?

In what ways can we rethink everything?

How do we work out exactly what is valuable from the past and what to drop?

What no longer serves us?

How do we know?

One of the fantastic qualities we human beings share is our ability to abstract. Abstraction in this sense, is taking ourselves out of a situation, separating ourselves from it, and imagining a different scenario than the one we currently occupy as we looked at in the chapter on creativity. This creative capacity allows for growing crops, cooking food, planning the future, crafting great art works and co-creating enlightened cultures.

When this awesomely creative capacity is mobilised through a self-construct with an un-evolved emotional intelligence, the result is either dissociated fantasy, planetary destruction or ugly barbarity.

The capacity to separate away from others, to increase the divide between subject and object and treat the 'other' with contempt and barbarity is pathological. Pathological dissociation is the shadow side of the potential of creative abstraction and can be termed sociopathy and even psychopathy.

Creative abstraction leads to art, music, literature and real civilisation. Creative abstraction leads people to treat their lives as if they were art. We revere and celebrate great creativity. I find it interesting that pathological dissociation and creativity are opposite poles of the same energy.

How do we move from pathology to goodness and beauty as a culture?

We currently create computer games, some of which entrain our younger generations brains in grotesque (virtual) behaviours such as robbery, murder and illicit activities.
Whilst this is purely neural and not actual, what does it do the neurology of its users?

Is this intelligent culture creation?

Shaming, abusing and neglectful childcare practices do not serve to create the most emotionally intelligent brains, they do not help to bring out the greatest potential in each of us.
When childcare is given such a low cultural priority, is this surprising?

People prioritise making money and profit over childcare, is this really an intelligent evolutionary strategy?

What are we to do about it?

I recommend Sue Gerhardt's work as a starter on this topic. Her first book Why Love Matters explores creating emotionally intelligent and astute brains, whilst her second book Selfish Society looks at how to create a culture of self-oriented indifference.

If we want a culture of selfishness then we co-create a culture where brain development leads to emotional dysfunction and feelings of separation and disconnection.
Is such a culture in any way sustainable?

Probably not.
Seeing some of the problems is a beginning.
A potent belief is that everyone ultimately wants love, tolerance and respect.
How might we choose to embrace and foster these natural desires and qualities, and more, within our culture?

How will we choose to educate our population about their minds, their emotional responses, their biology, psychology and global ecology,

whilst taking full responsibility for their own wellbeing and creative power?

Consequently, how do we choose, as a species, to build a world that is based on mutual love, respect, empowerment, vibrant creativity and ecological sanity?

Into the future...

I was standing outside the Buddhist centre in Newcastle in the UK before teaching a workshop, chatting to a bright young student.
Our conversation turned to the subject of culture creation. The architecture was grim. Red brick walls reached skywards as sharp edges in abrupt lines cut through space. A forest of metal bars created a prison like cage as grey tarmac surrounded the whole soul-less enterprise. This barren urban landscape had been brutally pushed from someone's mind, from their belief and values into our sensory fields.
They had dreamed into existence this ugly urbanity,
This was based on what?

On the culture creation they had been conditioned by and were ensconced in.
I asked the young student...
"Did you design this?"
The young man said...
"No of course not"
I replied...
"Neither did I. But what would it look like if you did?"
he smiled...
"Now that's a good question"

All of our world has come out of mind. Everything arises out of imagination and moves through mind into form.
But then where do the minds that had the vision for this oppressive city landscape arise from?

From their conditioning and the conditioning of those that conditioned them. Unless we are willing to rethink or more importantly dethink and deconstruct our conditioning, we will carry on what has always been done on some level or another.

People suffer from 'sick building syndrome'. This is where architecture dysfunctionally affects people's state of mind. People used to build with respect to the ratios of perspective found in nature such as phi and the fibonacci sequence. People also used to build in relation to the contours of the earth. Now we are living with the psychological and emotional consequences of the architectural legacies of the last half century. These legacies arise from the dissociation of church and science and the subsequent advance of post-modern, separatist materialism and how these philosophies affect peoples mind and perspective. If the quality of life is improved and facilitated by what we do let us continue it, if it isn't, lets change it.

Let's get really good measures of quality of life and prioritise this over measures of gross production or some other measure of consumption of limited resource. Let quality of life be the measure of our architecture or of our nutrition, of our work life and recreation, of our communities and our culture.

If we look at the world around us and contemplate how and why it is as it is, would we reproduce it that way or would we do something different?

Why aren't we doing something different?

These are worthy questions because if we understand the consequences of cultural conditioning and culture creation then we can begin to co-create something positively different, powerful and worthwhile for the quality of human life, for all our lives.

Conscious co-evolution invites us to deconstruct everything, re-think everything and if necessary re-create everything.

Let's co-create our culture and world from a place of bright creativity that really honours the holotropic perspective that recognises the inseparable nature of reality. Let's co-create means together in mutual relationship. This mutual relating has both systemic and integral qualities.

Systemic is the interwoven web of ecology.

Integral is the interwoven web of emptiness as form, form as emptiness.

We recognise that many people revere the psychopathic men who inhabit our history books. Many people love to construct and admire memorials to them, and to the wars that have been the highlight of so many of our social myths. We can find such statues littered around the major thoroughfares of any city. However there is a statue on a side street near the river Rhine in Dusseldorf, Germany, of a mother and child. The statue is a poetic and evocative celebration of mother love. ***Why are there not more statues like this and less of the pompous generals on their war horses?***

Why do we still choose to celebrate the atrocities of war and destruction in preference to celebrating love and simple humanity?

So when we become conscious of how we co-create culture and utilise these skills more fully and more collectively, what shape will our future have?

Maybe it will be the world according to some gruesome apocalyptic Hollywood fantasies, according to patriarchal Abrahamaic prophesies or maybe, just maybe it will it be something different.
What is your circle of influence?

What power do you have to co-create?

What are your choices for our collective future?

Shall we consciously co-create a culture that honours and celebrates all it's participants?

Concerted collective action as a force for change

the twenty-first key of conscious co-evolution is concerted collective action

The power of numbers is important. The more people who want specific change, the more it is likely to happen.
When we work with concerted and collective action, the synergy for change becomes unstoppable.
When an idea has reached it's time it is dreamt and acted, manifested into existence.
When there are enough seeking new ways, the tipping point is reached and everything shifts.
We are seeking the tipping point of enough people into practices of awareness and finding presence.

Enough people willing to take responsibility for their lives, their thought world, their emotional world and their bodies and health, are the tipping point.

Enough people seeking to move beyond the jaded vision of separatist, materialist consumerism are enough, the tipping point is reached.

Enough people laughing at the illusion of ownership of the planetary surface and living the vision of conscious co-evolution are the tipping point.

Enough people willing to steward this amazing planet and care for its resources and manifest species are enough, the tipping point is reached.

Enough people standing up and collectively denouncing the greed focused, fossil fuel driven nightmare of an economy are enough, the tipping point has been reached.

Enough people understanding, knowing and acting from the vision of conscious co-evolution and the tipping point is reached, the change has come.

Let's all make the difference that makes the difference.

The Inner Work - what kind of thing does it involve?

somatic practice - finding flow

A body-based practice is an important opportunity for cultivating embodied awareness. Embodied awareness is when we find awareness in the flesh and in the energy of movement. Somatic means 'of the living body' and it is an exploration of the intimacy of body, breath, bio-energy, mind and environment all through the lens of our direct experience.

A daily somatic practice of 20-60 mins is more than adequate. If you're going to teach somatic practice you probably need to do a whole lot more, but to make it work in your life 20-30 mins of intelligent practice is good enough.
An intelligent body-based practice keeps us well, is a practice of empowerment, preventative medicine and a celebration of incarnation. Somatic practice is mindful movement and will be part of the healing journey and the journey into deeper love, connection, awakening and freedom. It's an exploration of openness, integrated with strength, and woven with awareness into optimal function. Each flowing movement and moment of the mind-breath-energy-body is a gateway to realisation of the always-already inseparability, that is reality.

Awakening to reality, we will not need all our embodied ego defences, or the isolation and withdrawal strategies, held up by our unconscious yet lived beliefs about separation. The citadel of the self-structure eventually tumbles down, and somatic practice prepares for, invites and welcomes this inevitability.

Keeping the body as healthy and well as you can, can be seen as an act of worship or devotion, which. from a non-dual vision, is bio-philia. Learning to listen deep into the tissues, we take appreciative attention into the experience of tightness, contraction and unfeeling, which slowly yields to feelings of softness, fluidity, ease, joy and connected flow scintillating through our structure.

Listening in the body is through feeling, body-wisdom is finding awareness as feeling inside. As we feel inside, we cultivate somatic literacy and somatic intelligence, these are the pre-cursors to embodied awareness. Somatic practice is always in the awareness, not in capability or in the shapes being made.

The fascia of your body can be glued together, bound by hydrogen bonds, and when you seek to move them, sensation arises. The sensations of adhered fascial layers is discomfort and pain. Moving into discomfort and, resolving it into comfort and ease is a part of practice. Pushing into pain is incarnate ignorance and overwhelm for the nervous system. Pain is not listening, it is ego driven pushing to achieve some perceived goal. Somatic practice begins and ends with listening, mindful, appreciative listening and intelligent movement. Driving somatic practice as an extension of the ego's empire is nonsensical and dysfunctional. Listening is the beginning of wisdom and love. When adhered fascial layers start to release and flow the nerve endings that fire up are those of the pleasure receptors, the movement feels really good, it can feel joyful, blissful and facilitate a relaxed sense of presence and peace as well as alert engagement.

As we move more gracefully, we may also lose sense of the defined edges of our separate sense of existence. The flow of breath and the fractal edges of the body as well as the fuzzy nature of the electro-magnetic system all become potentially apparent and this temporarily relaxes and disinhibits the parts of our brain which normally generate our sense of solidity, definition and separation.

The sensations of peace, bliss and stillness that can arise lead naturally into silent sitting and meditation, and help us relax into the cosmos as if it were a friendly place. Somatic practice brings us home to our place on this planet, bring us back home to our bodies and their direct and inseparable connection to the planet and all of life.
Will we start stewarding this planet instead of suffocating it with toxic waste, poisoning its air and murdering it's myriad species with selfishness and consumerism, whilst we savage the climate so the sixth great extinction looks more and more imminent, caused by none other than us.
When will we start living like this wonderful biosphere is our home

and treat it with utmost respect and care?

Meditation - discovering core identity

Meditation changes how brains work and offers us a powerful transformational tool as our perceptual position shifts from self to no-Self, from personal to transpersonal, from selfishness to no-Self. This is sometimes called a 'turning about in the seat of consciousness'.
Being good at meditation itself is for stress relief. Being good enough at meditation, yet understanding it's deeper purpose, it becomes a vehicle serving the purpose of awakening, from the personal and the unreal to what is real.

In terms of practice, fifteen to twenty minutes of meditation practised twice daily is better than a long sit once a week. One long sit each week is better than none. Fifteen to twenty minutes of meditation practised twice daily plus one long sit each week is awesome. Build up organically to forty-five minutes or an hour if your life permits. Regularity, strategy and integration are far more important than intensity. Practising wisely, like this reaps results. Practising badly, with lack of regularity, doubt, grandiosity, falling into trance states or other delusions, reaps more suffering, so allow yourself to relax into practice. Avoid creating any narratives of 'who is practising' or how good the practices are and recognise that all you have to do is put in your best effort and be patient.

Meditation is simply paying attention to what's happening and choosing what to attend to. Choosing what to attend to is the strategy. The beginning practices are about simply sitting erect and comfortable and paying attention to the breath. You feel the inbreath and outbreath. You settle your mind into the breath and let it rest there. Attention will then most likely to shift to thinking, or maybe some body sensation and then into thinking about what that sensation means. It could shift into feelings and then stories about that feeling and so on. Attention often goes to future anticipation as well, what could happen next or mental rehearsals. All this movement of mind and attention as a facet of this is normal. The practice of meditation is simply to return the attention to the focus of attention, in this case, the breath. Meditation is about failing and in failing learn about who you really are.

Meditation firstly cultivates sustained witness consciousness. Finally it dissolves witness consciousness into the matrix of awareness and we find authentic freedom through this process.
Meditation is simple! If you believe meditation is hard work and super complicated and will take lifetimes to master then you will be right. If you believe meditation is natural and is a practice that you can work effectively and easily with, then you will also be right.

In *The Book of Purpose (2012)* by Christopher Gladwell, you'll find other strategies for the rapid development of meditational practice so that it facilitates the transparency of the self-contraction.

Priests, whatever their cult, like to overly complexify everything. This gives them authority and power. Being interested in mutual empowerment we will deconstruct mythology and share the essential qualities of practice so that it becomes available and accessible to all.
Meditation is simply the practice of not getting caught up. Not getting caught up means -

- We no longer get driven by the ancient parts of our neurology
- We no longer get caught up in feelings, we see them for what they are
- We no longer get caught up in thinking, ideas, concepts and mean ings, we see them for what they are.
- We no longer get caught up in our stories about what is happening

Meditation is the practice of presence. Being present, we no longer caught up. Finding and sustaining presence can be facilitated through mindfulness and practice.

The ancient parts of our neurology are the older facets of our informational systems that have come though evolutionary biology. These include the cellular informational systems inherited from simple single cellular lifeforms and the invertebrate brain of the enteric nervous system that functions through craving, aversion and ignorant indifference. This we can work with with particular somatic practices.

Our ancient neurology includes the brainstem inherited from our amphibian and reptilian ancestors, the feeding, fucking, fighting and freezing-in-fear brain, the brain of the four F's. This we can work with

with appropriate somatic and breath practices.

The older facets of our neurology include the proto-mammalian brain of primary emotions and the amygdala which registers traumatic emotional intensity and it's associated memories. We work with this brain in meditation, relaxation practices, emotional yoga and bodywork, through touching and being touched.

We also have the neo-mammalian cortex of rationality and conceptualisation, this we work with in meditation and relaxation.

Lastly we have our evolving neurology, arising through practice and beginning to be evidenced in empirical studies. This I call the disciplined brain.

With diligent practice the clarity arising through meditative awareness flows into the period of post-meditation and manifests as behaviour in the world. The vision of inseparability, knowing this through meditation, and acting in this way in the world become one flow of living clarity.

Entraining our brains through meditation and mindfulness changes how they work. Meditators brains work differently. We can cultivate a more active left pre-frontal cortex and states of gamma synergy. This means that the brain is more harmonised and we experience more non-contextual joy as the base line experience of life than is the norm. We also have a more refined executive control so we are less reactive to arising phenomena, including our ancient neurology and can be more responsive and creative.

Meditation also creates the direct experience of subjective depth and exposes the post-modern view that suggests all viewpoints are equal, through directly experiencing the meta-position of pristine awareness. In subjective depth we directly experience the seamless flow of everything being connected and the paradoxical position of inhabiting a separate feeling nervous system, we are one and many at the same time.

Meditation also dissolves the nihilistic view of pointlessness and the view of eternalism. Eternalists see everything as destined and meaningful (mostly to their own ego). Nihilists see no purpose or meaning anywhere. Astute meditators rest in the middle, between nihilism and eternalism.

Dream Yoga can accelerate the process of meditative awareness. Somatic Yoga can enhance and accelerate the process of meditative awareness.

Each of these three key practices, meditation, somatic practice and dream work, along with a basic understanding of yoga of the emotions work in synergy to weave insight and realisation through daily life and lead to an awakened life.

If we practice with integrity and diligence, vowing to use the energy of practice for the benefit of all beings everywhere, then practice is empowered, vital, energised and sparkles through the rest of life in unexpected ways.

Meditators craft purpose, rest happily in chance and probability, seek no sanctuary anywhere and know the meaning of life to be this precise moment.

self reflection and inquiry - Finding no-Self through the self

Ironic perhaps but the route to the freedom of the transpersonal is through the self-contraction, the ego. This self-sense finally leads us to the point of jumping off the cliff of rationality into the sanity of awakening.

The self-sense is the key point of leverage between selfishness and opening up to the vast open love of the no-Self. Either the self-sense looks down (I'm deliberately using the verticality metaphor here!) into the obsessions and concerns of the small self, or it begins to look up into the unbounded and vast reality of our core-identity.

I usually find it more helpful to teach in terms of depth and unfolding, but it's good to play with common cultural metaphors at times, even if they are largely unconscious. The up-down metaphor has a lot of currency, though seriously now, standing on the surface of a spherical planet, moving in space-time, in an expanding universe that may well be like the skin of a balloon, where, please tell me, exactly, is this mythical 'up' and where is it's polar opposite 'down'?

That aside for a moment. You have to get utterly bored and frustrated with being such a selfish, obsessive and small minded being, riddled with narcissistic obsessive traits. You have to see enough of your ego strategies of separation, deceit, manipulation and coercion to want something more. You have to believe there is something more than being just a healthy ego. And you have to have the desire to change and grow.

The neuroses of the ego are the twists of realised energy. The realised energy of our true nature is distorted through the conditioning we received as a child, and through our culture. This true nature has been twisted through fear into ultimate concern only for one's own welfare, and the welfare of one's ethnic group and culture.

Openness to love becomes jaded through the boundaries we impose on life, so all that remains underneath every opening into love is firstly fear of loss and then even more fear and separation.

If we study our neuroses and follow their energy deeply enough we will see that every neurotic feeling and thought is bubbling out of the illusion of being a separate self-sense.

Once we realise that all our stories and all our fears are no more than twisted bubbles of dualistic distortion, we have to want more. The alternative of going for more is to collapse into the post-modern disease of nihilistic desperation, depression or existential crisis.

The deeper feelings of love and the recognition of underlying consciousness moving through our neuroses and obsessive self-stories sustains us through our dark nights of the soul. I've had my fair share of these and wouldn't wish them on anyone. Yet in some way, as long as we can stay open to grace, these dark nights of the soul serve to free us up. They serve in enabling us to honour our own shadow and darkness, reclaim it and through this find integration, balance and transparency. The energy of the drive to realisation, the natural goodness in us of awakened potential guides us through the dance of shadow and light until we begin to recognise that being nobody is the way to love. Nobody walks the path to love and there is no path to love, there is only this moment of openness. When we're happy being no-body, being inconsequential, nobody going nowhere, only then we can be somebody. We are reborn through grace. The dawn of love only comes after the deep dark night of pain, struggle, loss and desperation.

- Wisdom teaches us we are nobody.
- Love teaches us we are everybody.

Love-compassion and wisdom-clarity in action is conscious co-evolution in daily life. As compassion and clarity in action, we act spontaneously in the best possible way for the benefit of all beings, we don't have to contrive it, practising goodness is over. The natural goodness of our innate nature dances as the light of awareness through the twists and cracks of our transparent self-story, exactly as it needs to. Spontaneously arising goodness for the benefit of all beings just happens, all of the time.

relaxation - being present with what is

Recreation is important. The capacity and the opportunity to relax into life is crucial to wellbeing, continued creativity, and real enjoyment.

Recreation that is sensitive enough to the lives of other people and members of other species is switching on to enlightened process.
How do you relax and re-create in an eco-intelligent manner?
- Play music
- Dance
- Sit by the ocean
- Surf
- Sail
- Paraglide
- Paint
- Walk in the woods and mountains
- Practice parkour
- Climb
- Run
- Drive ecologically destructive internal combustion engines at furious speed, killing wildlife and eroding the remaining countryside?

Part of a quality lifestyle of weaving conscious co-evolution into everyday life is to facilitate relaxation and recreation for all. The balance of the sympathetic and parasympathetic nervous systems is crucial for wellbeing, it is crucial for creativity.

Our culture is dependent on creativity, creativity is enhanced by appropriate amounts of relaxation. Great inventions often occur in daydreams. Kekule discovered the benzene ring, the chemical structure of benzene discovered by the German chemist August Kekule. after dreaming of a snake eating its own tail, just like the great mythic serpent Ouroboros. Ouroboros represents infinity, the eternal cycle of life, death, time and space as well as the movement of the sun. Einstein discovered the principle of relativity after dreaming of riding on a sunbeam. Crick and Watson apparently discovered the alpha helix shape for DNA after dreaming of two snakes spiralling around each other. Samuel Taylor Coleridge composed one of his romantic epics titled Kubla Khan after an opium inspired dream. Sir Paul McCartney dreamed up the melody for the beautiful song 'Yesterday', which contains the lyrics "When all my troubles seemed so far away, yes I believe in..."

President Abraham Lincoln dreamed of his death a few days prior to the event. It is tradition in some indigenous cultures for the elders to dream of the time of their death and to then walk out into the wilderness to meet their death, at peace and alone. Some mathematicians, including the great Ramanujan, dreamt up works inspired by a muse, or as is said in Ramanujan's case, a feminine deity. Chuang-Tzu, the fourth century (CE) Taoist philosopher from China, dreamed of being a butterfly dreaming it was a human being dreaming of being a butterfly... So arose much contemplation on the nature of mind and meaning. How much more art, science, and philosophy is inspired by daydreams?

What do your daydreams inspire you to do or be?

How will you allow recreation to be your platform from which to co-create?

What will you dream into existence?

A conscious culture is one in which creativity plays a large part and which celebrates and creates space and time for relaxation, recreation and creativity. The suppression of creativity to drive an unsustainable and economically unsound culture serves no-one. Seriously it serves no-one, not even those who think they may benefit.

So lets learn to relax deeply and find more expansive creativity, it is our birthright and our purpose to be creative and inspired. It is these attributes that add quality to life and make a life of quality.

Power Siesta

Power Siesta is, most simply, an enhanced siesta. It is a way of resting deeply within a state of rejuvenative deep relaxation.

Power Siesta is a method of releasing stress, resolving stress or remaining stress free. Stress is the embodiment of the experience of separation, Power Siesta assists you dropping this illusion.

Power Siesta is brief and effective, workable for busy lives.

Power Siesta allows you to be more effective in whatever your chosen livelihood and lifestyle is.

Power Siesta is another method that can be utilised to keep you in a positive flow, capable of responding with clarity to the arising needs and demands of life.

This practice has nineteen simple, rejuvenating steps, enjoy them...

- Sit in a chair or, even better, lie down.

- Now allow your mind to rest, drop deeply into the body, we utilise the briefest periods of time to drop into deep relaxation to revitalise and re-energise.

- Now, as rapidly as you can, drop your awareness through the layers of muscles and bones. Feel their living heaviness, rest your mind in this feeling and now, let them all be. Let them go with your mind, back into earth, returning, for the duration of this practice to the element from which they arose.

- Drop your awareness through the layer of organs and into the fluid feeling of pulsing blood, lymph and water. Feel the fluid body, its rhythms and tides. Take your mind deep into this pulsation. Rest here comfortably, and now let them all be. Let them go with your mind, back into the oceans, back to the rivers, the water element from which they arose.

- Drop your awareness into the heat of the body. Feel the fire produced from burning glucose in the cells. Recognise that this glucose came through plants, originally from sunlight. Feel the fire of the body, rest comfortably in this, and now let it be, let it all go. Let the fire go with your mind, back into the fires of the cosmos.

- Drop your awareness into the breath, feel your attention rest deep in the subtle nuances of the movement of gases in your body. Feel these gases permeate all your cells, one flow with the atmosphere around you. Feel the movement of the winds moving through you and rest comfortably in this, and now let it all be. Let the breath go, just for the duration of this practice, let it go with your mind, let it go back into the vast open skies from where it came.

- Now rest your attention into the space within and between breaths. Find awareness in the space between thoughts, the space between cells, the space between atoms, and the vast open space inside of atoms. Feel the space your body is in, and the space that is your body. Now relax into space, be awareness, one with space, let everything go that no longer serves you and the greatwr good, let it go with your mind. Relax into space, gone, completely gone.

- Allow yourself to rest, cradled by the supporting universe. Dissolve into luminosity, as luminosity. Resting deeply as this, feel only peace and pure-being-ness, utterly vast, empty, yet full, blissful radiance.

- Rest as long as you need to here, in the timeless, space-less void. Gradually and creatively reformulate, recreate your 'self' and feel space in and around you. Allow space. Breathe space, be space.

- Move your attention into your neurology - the brain, the spinal cord, the nerves and synapses, the vibrant web of living sentience that you are. Be aware also of your patterns of thinking, believing, feeling and action, and find spaciousness and peace and with these. Allow vi brant sentience.

• Move your attention to the breath and feel the subtle ecstasy of the inhale and exhale. Feel the wind invigorate your existence bringing ease and grace. Allow wind.

• Bring your attention to the fires, the furnaces of life, in every cell cele brate joyfully the living sun of your body. Allow fire.

• Feel deeply the swelling waves of the ocean of this body as it pulses and flows. Let your mind dance in response to the powerful waves of life juic es and passions. Allow water.

• Let your mind settle deeply into the mountains of earth, crystal caverns and verdant fertile woods that are the organs, muscles and bones. Allow your mind to sing with gratitude and presence. Allow earth.

• With your next out breath begin moving these muscles, from the periph ery, move gently and feel mind as muscle, softly reclaim their power and fluidity.

• Feeling fully incarnate, at ease, comfortable in existence, find endless energy and resource, rejuvenation, creativity and vital living connection.

• Decide to fully awaken now, feeling energised, resourced, rejuvenated, revitalised and ready to continue your day.

• Take in a deep breath, then breathing slowly and richly out with the sound Aaaah, Awaken.

• Enjoy each arising moment of life.

vibrational practice - it's all vibration

Mantra is a yogic practice of vibration and it literally means mind expansion, and can also mean mind protection. A mantra practice uses sound and vibration to explore our neural webs and tissues and our nature as vibration. As we chant and make sound we feel our osmotic boundaries with the world around and experience greater peace, clarity and connection.

- Mantra as vibration invites the expansion of small mind into vast potential.
- Mantra as vibration offers protection from one's own mundane and tedious self-story.

Mantra as vibration is first practised aloud. This needs to occur often enough to get the mantra charged with vitality and for the mind and body systems to become deeply familiar with its vibration.
The vibration becomes neurologically entrained through practice.
Remember when we are practising, we are exploring vibration and the vibrational matrix of existence.
Since mantra is used by religions, and rightly so as it is a potent practice, it is possible to get snared in the accretions of religion. In my view, any religion worth it's salt will take its exegetes as rapidly as possible beyond the ossification of exoteric dogma into the esoteric essence of its methods and into authentic freedom. Used in this way to internalise into greater freedom, working with vibration is always about touching vast potential, not about falling into the pit of dogma.

Later, mantra as vibrational practice can be done as a whisper on the breath.
Lastly, mantra as vibrational practice can be done silently in the mind whilst deepening the breath.

Mantra is energy, it is vibration and it allows you to explore vibration and the mental generation of energy forms. We can use chanting or sound from any tradition or no-tradition to explore vibration.
Formal practices of vibration are done sitting with a beginning and an end to the practice period. They will be done in specific settings such as shrine rooms, meditation spaces, and so on.
Informal practices are where the vibration spontaneously generates itself, and can occur literally anywhere, in any situation. Informal practices are rooted in formal practices. Silent practice is rooted in audible practice. The vibration slowly gains power through repetition.

Focusing life energy and attention on the vibration instead of on one's

relentless self-story, is a developmental delight. A person who can stop cerebral noise, cease involvement at will with inner dialogue and rest in the inner space with only the hum of vibration is close to freedom.
The person who can then allow the vibration to softly dissolve in consciousness and then rest in boundless emptiness, is free.
Weaving emptiness, energy and form as inseparability through vibration into life is the work of conscious co-evolution.
Chanting and singing then becomes an act of generosity and love.

Vibrations condensed into sounds that have effects but no intrinsic meaning are my preference as we avoid the accretions of religion in this way. These vibrations create ripples in the heart and mind, ripples that create moods, feelings, mind states and states of connection as a step beyond our limitations into new possibility.
Each vibration has a particular quality that we can feel into and use for our greater good and the greater good of all. Vibration used wisely can be used to supplant the self-references of our self-sense and thus undermine this mythological narrative of 'self' and it's obsessions.
Going deeper than this narrative, we find deep peace beyond any identification. This practice is profoundly liberating and is related to the ancient tantric practice of nyasa mentioned previously.

Vibration is a means to...
Create shift and change in energy
Craft new neurological possibilities
Know the vibrational nature of existence
Remember the body as sacred
Remember what is true and real
Bring the self-sense to transparency

Working with vibration is a slow, deep and powerful practice that is inexorable in its power and capacity to remind us of the depths of existence.

ethical base - helps us compute seamlessness

From now on we can choose to...

1. Cultivate awareness and kindness internally as much as possible and take personal responsibility for all thoughts, feelings, projections, choices and the consequences of these in your inner life.

2. Cultivate as much awareness and kindness in your external behaviours as possible and be aware of the choices available.
Take full responsibility for your actions and choices and the effects of these in your relationships and life.

3. Study existence and grow knowledge of the inter-relatedness, inseparability and non-inherence of all things.
Choose to act from this place of wisdom. Choose to continue to inquire into the nature of life, from the appearance of subjective and objective perspectives with all the tools available to you.

4. Practice, explore and cultivate wonder, joy, contentment, playfulness, empowered resilience, generosity, gratitude, love, will, surrender, relaxation, bliss, real wealth, wisdom, impeccable positivity and authentic freedom.
Choose sublime contentment and wonder with arising phenomena, let them flow as they do, without gripping, fear or ignorant indifference.

5. Choose to get comfortable with paradox.

6. Choose to cultivate devotion to life, life-force and inseparable totality and see the core truth of every being's existence as naturally free and good.

7. Choose to experience, know and communicate from deep truth, beyond any relative agendas of subjective truth.

8. Choose to recognise if you behave in ways that hurt either others or yourself.
Choose to learn as quickly as possible and aim not to repeat any hurtful intentions, thoughts, speech or behaviours. Choose to effectively learn and accelerate your learning curve whilst minimising toxic guilt, shame and blame.
Remember there is no sin, no right and no wrong.
Remember there is simply unskilful thinking, speaking and behaving,

or, there is skilful thinking, speaking and behaving.
Know that unskilful behaviour hurts others and your own awakening.
Know that skilful behaviour helps all find joy and the roots of joy in awakening and allows the planet and its myriad species to thrive.
Choose to cultivate skilfulness and forgive yourself for past unskil-ful-ness.

9. Choose to celebrate and honour the arising energy of awakening in all beings including yourself.

10. Choose to drop guilt, shame and blame and other unproductive, irresponsible and unskilful toxic mind states.
Adults seeking to control our life energies in unhealthy ways conditioned these toxic states into us as children. Dropping these states choose to free yourself. Guilt is temporarily helpful if it helps us to learn. Shame is toxic. Blame misunderstands the nature and inter-related complexity of reality and responsibility.

11. Choose to breathe well and laugh often.

12. Choose to celebrate creativity and make life your art.

These are the twelve ethical choices and practices for the cultivation of authentic freedom.

The Twelve Choices in Practice

These twelve choices when put into practice, consistently work for the greatest and most evolutionary good.
Using our minds, emotions, bodies, actions and lives in ways that support this vision is extremely powerful.
Even if at times we are unsure what this greatest good might look or feel like, we can sustain a powerful intention to enable this 'greater good' to become manifest, knowing its essential elements of kindness and love, intelligence, clarity and wisdom, deep peace, bliss, presence, joy and authentic freedom for all.
This vision of the 'greater good' activated through these choices, is the win-win-win ethical foundation from which all mind training and visioning can thrive. In win-win-win behaving, you win, others win and the whole planet wins. This is advanced eco-ethics.

Everything we create in our life begins in dreams and imagination, it then moves through the power of desire, is mediated by belief and manifested through motivation and appropriate creative collaborative action.
We can of course continue to create unconsciously and have no real developed skills in this area, in which case we simply recreate our unconscious patterns, shadows and past history.

One could, however, choose to pay attention to possibilities of how to develop these skills. With the key developmental skills in place, one could easily move through unconscious-incompetence into conscious-incompetence. Our wise choice from conscious-incompetence is always to develop any necessary skills and move through the practice of these skills towards conscious competence. This classic chain of embodiment runs through unconscious-incompetence through conscious-incompetence to effort oriented-competence summating in effortless competence.

Real skilfulness is effortless-competence, by which time skills have become deeply applied, embedded and embodied in everyday life.
Of course we can also choose to continuously update our skills and become ever more proficient. Learning to learn and continuing to sharpen one's learning is skilful.

Unskilful processing is our enemy, not any external trigger. Difficult internal processing creates a dramatic illusion out of the experiences of our lives, an illusion we are ultimately, totally responsible for creating and freeing our selves from.
Change, growth and authentic freedom arises when we risk everything, cease taking anything personally, take total responsibility and, above all, cultivate a big sense of humour.

From this base we can become involved with the exploration of all aspects of our life and start to let go of every psycho-emotional fabrication.
Anything less is less. So lets awaken, lets find authentic freedom.

If, every time we begin any practice or sit in meditation we invoke the

four qualities of …
- Always-already seamlessness
- Intelligence-wisdom-clarity
- Love-compassion-kindness
- Authentic freedom for all beings

Then we direct the practices to transcend the self-contraction and find conscious co-evolution.

If, every time we finish our mat practice or sitting in meditation we dedicate the energies and qualities arising through practice for the benefit of all beings everywhere, then we begin the process of directing the practice to transcend the self-contraction and find conscious co-evolution.
And now, we can start to make these practices, action in our daily life.

emotions and feelings

Feelings and emotions are mind in the body, they're a form of communication. Feelings and emotions begin in body sensations, they're felt initially as sensations, we then attribute meanings to those collections of sensations. If we can fully feel and feel into these emotions with the eye of awareness we can start to deconstruct the emotions and see what they are made up of.

Emotions are the primary affective experiences, feelings are secondary, they are what happens when we have ascribed meaning.
What are these sensations and emotions saying to you though, what are they communicating?

Feelings and emotions give us two key pieces of information and then the flavour or quality of that.

- They tell us we feel separate or connected.
- They tell us the flavours or feelings of that connection or separation.

Feelings of separation	**Feelings of connection**
Hatred	Loving
Jealousy	Compersion
Envy	Generosity
Fear	Courage
Anxiety	Connected, at one
Greed	Contentment
Anger	Clarity
Confusion	Purposeful

and so on.. you get the concept.
Emotions are hard to work with as their 'tones' are so compelling. They are immediate and quite pressing, sometimes even explosive. Yet if we can be fully with them, whilst not being them, They will change.
As we see them change, and we know them more intimately as internal meteorology about the nature of connection or separation then they lose their power.
We can also understand that actually we are never not connected. All there is is connection.
So gradually difficult feelings are deconstructed and seen for what they are and lose their power to drive our lives. We become the architect of the emotions and feelings rather than them being the commandant of our lives.

We can feel feelings, own them, honour them, express them, act them out, medicate them or project them.

Acting out is when we live the feeling in the world.
Medicate them is when we take substances or do things to get rid of the feeling, work, sex, alcohol, drugs, thinking etc..
Project them we've looked at.
Express them is like saying, I am feeling angry! without acting out the anger..
Feel them, honour them, express them and then deconstruct and transform them is the route of wisdom.

When we stop trying to run away from our emotions and feelings, stop acting them out, or stop medicating them and really be with them, then we see them change. We see them rise, grow, reduce and dissolve away into another feeling which also rises, grows, reduces and dissolves away, each one trying to tell us how separate we are or how connected we are.

As we practice our breathing practices we get that we are only ever connected, so the feelings of separation are believed less and less until their power dissolves.

Let's look at three quite difficult feelings of separation to work with, anger, anxiety and depression. This will give you an idea of how pervasive they can be to start with and how they can resolve.

Anger

Anger is rooted in powerful sensations and is potentially a powerful motivating energy, but it needs to be mastered. Anger is one of the hardest emotions to work with as it is so fast, so explosive that to have the witness space, the awareness space to be able to work with the rapid sensations and our reaction to those requires a high level of meditative skill, but it can be done, bit by bit.

Where does anger come from?

Often it arises because someone did something we didn't want them to do. We expected A and B happened. It is our unconscious expectations that were frustrated. Yet they were unconscious! We don't see them, don't know them and don't communicate them. How can anyone be expected to mind read our unconscious expectations. Anger rises from lack of clarity. If we are clear about our desires and needs then anger never rises in personal offence.

Anxiety

Anxiety is pernicious, it eats away at our energy and our capacity to be present.

The thing with anxiety is it is a kind of relentlessly present sensation with subtle but continuously present fear about the future. Yet, the future isn't happening.

It's a learnt pattern, maybe from our parents who also would have 'done' anxiety. However it arose, it gets into your guts and sits there like

a worm eating your life, your hope and your dreams.
When you feel anxious. Ask yourself - “Is this that I fear happening?” The answer is No, because what we fear is in the future and the future is not here.
To deal with anxiety we practice all the practices we have learnt and practice micro practices that act as a pattern interrupt every time the anxiety grabs us and threatens to eat our life.
Gradually we feel the fear and keep doing it anyway, we get up, we do what we have to do and as we sit each day the feelings gradually gradually fade away and we are free to live our life and manifest our dreams.

Depression
Depression is compelling, a creeping black fog, a stinking black dog that sits on our hearts and cramps all movement. Depression is like a sick vine that wraps up the past in rotting foliage and sends its tendrils into the future obscuring the sun. The present is rotten and empty and the future is just a slow way to death. This is depression, I’ve been there.
Ask yourself
What is real?

Practice the micro practices that act as a pattern interrupt and feel your body. Feel the earth underneath you.
Is the future happening?

No.
What is real?

Just this breath this moment of the body.
Breathe in the good, breathe in the sunshine, the colour of flowers, a smile everything that sings of goodness and let if good your system.
Practice gratitude, however, to whatever, for breath, for food, for sunshine, for everything. Gratitude gradually clears depression, gratitude is good medicine. Gratitude clears the sky of fog and allows the sun to be seen.
Practice with your emotions and feelings, watch them rise, grow, reduce and dissolve away. Study your feelings like you would a lover. Feel them but don’t be them. Refuse to act those feelings out. Practice micro practices that act as a pattern interrupt at any time to reduce their intensity, if necessary. Look directly at your emotions and feelings and

understand them as messages of feeling connected or feeling separated.

Emotional practices assist you feeling the arising emotional experience of being separate and resting with the emotion until it resolves back into emptiness and unicity. All emotions change and dissolve, when we know this from the inside, difficult emotions can feel less problematic even if still very intense. Remember emotions are like body-thoughts, they carry information about survival and threat, about connection and separation, about worth and value. We facilitate emotional clarity when we practice body based and sitting practices daily. We can then fully rest into an emotion, like watching a rain storm on a windy day, and then watch it pass. The emotions of realisation that unfold are clarity, love, compassion and joy.
Wrath may arise but its centre is still clarity and compassion.
Wrath is non-personalised compassionate anger, it's a clear expression of the need for transformation. For example; if some greedy, psychopathic groups of men in control of global resource were ignorantly destroying our life-support system of the planet, wrath might be a highly appropriate response, what are your thoughts?

thought-forms - patterns of mind

When you were an embryo of around 21-24 days old you were three layers in an elongated oval disc. These three layers were the foundational layers of cells that led to the...

- Outside of your structure, the skin
- The muscles and bones
- The internal organs

These three layers are called the ectoderm, mesoderm and endoderm respectively. The ectoderm became your skin, the mesoderm your muscles and the endoderm your internal organs.
Then something happened!
The outer layer, the ectoderm started to push inwards along a long line on the top side, the ectodermal side of this oval disc.
This invagination pushed right into the disc and separating from the outer layer, bubbled through and created an inner core destined to

become the brain and spinal cord.

Not only that, but this neural core then sends shoots out to reach to all the other three layers. Each shoot goes to its genetically pre-specified location uniting central nervous system, organs, muscles, bones, fascia and skin in an endless web of inter-communication. The neural core and the layers of structure are inseparably engaged in neuro-chemical and genetic dialogue to create the complexity of the neuro-endocrine-somatic system which is the communicative, structural web that is your living body.

So the brain and spinal cord were originally that which became 'skin'. The eyes, ears and all other sense organs are modified skin cells too. Stroke your skin, its the outside of your brain. Go on do it again!

Despite the fact that the brain and central nervous system (CNS) as its function, mind, can feel separate to body, it really isn't, there is no separation. This is why we do somatic practices as well.

Breath initiates this process of reunification of awareness, body, mind and environment. Your physical practices of mindful movement include feeling into the body, activating and releasing muscles whilst breathing consciously continues this work. This deep inward feeling, seeing and listening into the body I like to call 'in-knowing'. This word is from Stranger in a strange land.. by Robert A Heinlein.. those that remember that fabulous book.

To truly relax and rest in awareness and awaken to the oneness of bodymind you have to know yourself as a unified whole, not fragmented pieces.

- Mammalian brains evolved out of reptilian brains.
- Reptilian brains evolved out of amphibian brains.
- Amphibian brains evolved out of fish brains.
- Fish brains evolved out of invertebrate brains.
- Invertebrate brains evolved out of protozoan levels of sentience.

Cellular sentience - all our cells are vital and alive and sensory - they need oxygen, nourishment, touch and movement amongst others things.

Our enteric brain - is what we inherited from being invertebrates. It has two primary emotive drives, wanting and withdrawal. Desire and aversion. This brain starts at the lips and finishes at the anus and wraps the whole of the intestines in a lace of nerves.
What helps this brain work well?
Fasting at times, and not eating too much.
Good diet, keeping your microbes happy by not eating sugar and highly processed foods.
Movement, it loves moving and resting deeply, a balance is needed.
Good breathing keeps the ENS out of fear.

Our reptile brain - arose from when we made the transition from water to earth. We had to breathe air and separate orifices had to arise. Fish can eat and breath through the same orifice, we can't. This brain controls breathing, eating and basic processes. It is often called the fucking, fighting, freezing, fleeing and breathing brain as this is what it governs. It is reptilian. We have somatic practices to train this dragon.

Emotional brain - arising from our early mammalian ancestry, it does the feelings we have looked at of separation and connection. It keeps us in the pack and stops us getting eaten through being separated and exiled.

Our cognitive brain - has two sides the spatial and the rational, right and left hemispheres respectively. This high brain is also the seat of our beliefs and our sense-of-self and shadow self. It gives us our rational thinking self, our story telling and meaning making.

Our disciplined brain. This is the trained brain. The brain that gives us the capacity to authentically make choices. This is the brain that allows us to shift brain wave states. Without brain training all that acts is our ancient biology. Ancient biology runs on algorithms and they are reflexive. Choice comes when we no longer act reflexively but can operate from choice.
Thats six different qualities to mind we are working with…
When we meditate we create space for choice. Space between stimulus and reflex, and in this creative space is the possibility of a new way of being, a new choice.

Discipline of witness consciousness, cultivated through attentional focus, gives us the capacity to build choice. Without witness stamina we are drawn into the old biology of sensations in the guts or of capitulating to emotions and feelings, or believing in the more recent biology of stories we hold dear, and beliefs and then we react from those places. With brain training we have freedom of choice.

With even more brain training, when our brains buzz with gamma synergy, we don't even have to make that choice. The choice is made. We know the limits of our ancient biology and none of it holds sway over our actions. At this point, brain training has done it's work.
You've got an untrained mind that dominates your life, what does this cost you?

We know that belief, utilising placebo, heals diseases.
We also know that belief, utilising nocebo (Mind causing pain) causes diseases.
Untrained minds moving rampantly through unskillful beliefs, solidity and separation cause suffering, disease, poor relationships and environmental desecration.

How do we work with this?
First - understand our mind
Second - we train the mind

So let's understand our mind.
Mind is simply what brains do, they are aware, think and reflect.
The evolution of the human brain is to aid our survival and reproduction, they do this well.
We're social mammals, so we need a mechanism to know where we are in terms of status, community relations and pecking orders.
This mechanism for us is storytelling, our brains make up stories and all these stories revolve around this deep feeling in us of 'ME'.
This 'ME' is a vortex of memories, feelings and stories that itself has the deep 'I' feeling at its core.
This 'ME' has a territory of 'MINE'

Firstly we have to acknowledge this and say YES, this is how it is, we

find acceptance. This gives us the capacity to look into this biology without fear. It's just how it is, for everyone. We are an 'I-ME-MINE' thing.
We need to honour this as well, it is beautiful, all our memories, all our stories, all our value and beliefs and thought forms are beautiful and fallible.
It is their fallibility that enables us to see through them.

Let's understand how we make up our memories and our stories.
We have five external senses.
These senses are limited.
Bees sense in ultra-violet, snakes in infra-red, sharks in patterns of electricity, squid in colour, dogs have forty times our capacity to hear.
All senses including our senses are just ways to interpret the vibrational matrix.
We have five channels to interpret the vibrational nature of the universe.
They're all partial and limited, they give us a fraction of the information about things, enough to survive.
With memory it is then the limits of what we pay attention to that we remember.
What do we pay attention to?

Mostly what our parents and schools taught us to pay attention to.
Then we remember the bits we paid attention to of the limited information from the sense fields and conjure up a story about it, this we then say is 'the truth, the whole truth and nothing but the truth'
Really?

Then every time we remember the memory we change it before putting it back into our memory banks. Memory is fallible. It is a story we tell ourselves.

The next thing brains do is make up meanings.
To survive into the future we use our memories, what appears to have happened and correlate that with what appears to be happening now (this just means, what we are paying attention to) and join all the dots of our experience to make up a meaning.
We rarely use science, we use how we feel about things or people, we

use what our culture told us to believe about things or people and we use the stories our mind has created as the glue from which we craft our meanings.

From our meanings about how the universe works and why, we create things we value and our beliefs.

Beliefs are consolidated meanings that drive our actions, relationships, and thoughts.

Minds are biological phenomena, what brains do, that make up an 'I-ME-MINE' feeling, which has limited changeable memories, fallible stories, meanings crafted from very fragmentary information, and we operate from beliefs that are the consolidation of these processes into a personalised operating system (POS).

Would you trust such a mechanism to tell you the truth?

No

So why do you?

Second - start to train the mind

We are going to train our brains, train our minds to be fully present, in the here and now, not operating from partial beliefs, fallible stories, fragmentary information, partial meanings, deluded memories or dubious meanings. This is the inner work.

What are beliefs again?

We've looked a little at beliefs as meanings consolidated into an operating system.

How can we soften belief and yet use it's power?

What is the power of belief?

The power of belief is seen in placebos.

We buy into a meta-narrative, a big overarching story about how something works and then suspend our rational mind. In that suspension we seem to be able to do some quite amazing things. When we suspend rational mind in this way and the power of belief kicks in and something 'miraculous' happens like a sudden cure from some disease.

Mind is powerful clearly, belief is one way it moves.

In a trained brain we are seeking to maintain the power of belief without belief being consolidated. If we can be what I call a 'belief artist', then we change our beliefs according to whatever new information is arising. The beliefs do not require consolidation but are worn lightly like loose fitting garments.
Start a practice of asking yourself..
What do I believe about this?

What else could I believe?

What is most useful, for the greatest good of all, to believe?

What limitations of belief do you have?

Can you change the beliefs you have?

Can you watch the situation change as you believe differently?

Changing beliefs at the bare minimum will change your mental and emotional filters towards what is possible and you will see new opportunities where previously there appeared to be only limits.
Become a belief artist.

sleep and dreams

We spend a third of our lives asleep. Sleep is very precious. Recognising that sleep is also a place where sentience occurs allows us to begin to extend the practice of awareness into the realm of sleep.
Being sleep deprived, however, leads to arousal of the stress systems and can lead to all manner of dis-eases so we don't want to reduce the quality of rest when we sleep.
Through awakening beyond the self-contraction, it is reported by many teachings and schools of practice, that the needs for sleep reduce. Sleep is a place where we appear to process emotion and consolidate memory, regulate our neurology and de-stress. If we identify fully with sentience rather than with the flows and changes of mind and feeling then it becomes less likely that we need to de-stress, process emotion or regulate our neurology in the same way. There is little research into the

relationships between awakening through meditative practice and sleep at the moment though.
Sleep does appear to be either on or off to us. Brains can be both at the same time though. Many creatures sleep uni-hemispherically, meaning they sleep on one side of their brain. Creatures such as dolphins, seals and birds have one hemisphere alert and one resting. This is probably an evolutionary strategy that facilitates survival. After all, when one is asleep one is highly vulnerable to becoming lunch.

Complex changes occur in the brain during sleep, as is evidenced by electro-encephalograms. After about ten minutes of resting in alpha brainwaves we go into a phase called non-rapid eye movement sleep - NREM.
NREM can be usefully divided into three stages.

1. NREM1 - light sleep with irregular, shallow brainwaves.
2. NREM2 - bursts of rhythmic brainwaves, spindles and k-complexes
3. NREM3... slow, deep 'delta' brainwaves.

Stage one is the lightest sleep, whilst stage three is considered to be deeper than the previous two stages.
After going through these NREM stages we go into rapid eye movement (REM) sleep.
The electroencephalogram (EEG) measures brain activity and during REM sleep is similar to that of drowsiness or even wakefulness. REM sleep is the stage where dreams most commonly occur.
A night's sleep usually consists of four to six of these cycles of NREM and REM sleep.

During sleep, there is usually also a reduction in heart rate of around ten beats per minute as well as a small fall in core temperature of around one to one and a half degrees centigrade. There is naturally a general reduction in movement and sensation. The motor and sensory activity of the nervous system in almost completely shut down, we are much less aware of the world around us and mostly incapable of movement until we awaken. Theories of sleep suggest it offers us a means of saving energy, a method for regulating emotions, provides us with information processing periods, allows memory consolidation, and much more.

It may be that sleep allows for the regulation of autonomic activity such as heart rate and in fact sleep disorders are often associated with autonomic nervous system dysfunction such as a disordered heart rate.

Another theory is that sleep alters the firing of nerve cells and changes the connectivity between networks of our neural cells. It is theorised that this occurs through altering the timing and synchronisation of firing across these network connections.

The central biological clock that sets circadian rhythms in conjunction with light levels certainly affects sleep timing. Light affects cells in the retina of the eye, which synchronises the biological clock and affects other brain areas associated with alertness. Light suppresses production of the sleep producing hormone melatonin. The pressure to fall asleep when one has been very active is through the effects of a neuro-modulator called adenosine.

Working with computers, watching TV screens, and exposure to city lights and domestic lighting will all affect the quality of one's sleep. It is better to switch off as much as possible and be quiet for an hour or so before sleeping to allow quality sleep.

Sleep at night is of a much better quality than daytime sleep. Sleep periods are shorter in the day, the REM periods that increase as sleep progresses during the night-times decrease during daytime sleep. This means that we benefit less from the dream periods during daytime sleep and we usually feel less well rested. The sleep spindles in NREM sleep are also more abundant at night, these are implicated in memory consolidation so this occurs less in daytime sleep. Because of these and other changes, night shift workers stand higher risks of cardio-vascular diseases, diabetes and other conditions.

Sleep deprivation is found to be an aspect of many psychiatric conditions. One theory is that the amygdala, which regulates mood and anxiety levels and is involved in the perception of threat, is activated more in sleep-deprived people.

Deep sleep and REM sleep help with the management of the plasticity of neural networks. These effects from REM sleep could, therefore, help with the acquisition of new skills and learning.

Studies of longevity find that those who live longest report sleeping between six and seven and a half hours per night. Women sleep longer than men and are also reported to enjoy a deeper quality of sleep. Women, on average, also live to an older age than men.

Practice relaxation before sleep and you will most probably rest deeper and your brain will more fully reap the benefits of sleep.

Remember that using computers, watching TV screens and sitting in bright artificial light before sleep will reduce the quality of rest and make it harder to sleep deeply and harder to get the best benefit from your sleep.

A practice of reviewing and reflecting on your day mentally and resolving any unresolved issues before sleep is also a sound way of deepening your sleep experience. As the old adage says "Don't sleep on an argument".

Siestas or Power Siestas are also a very good idea. Twenty to forty minutes of rest after lunch in the afternoon facilitates good digestion and allows for a level of rejuvenation that carries one through the afternoon and evening with ease. Many people seek to navigate the post-prandial energy drop by eating carbohydrates, sugar and drinking coffee.

Another useful strategy is to decide before going to sleep that you are going to rest well, when you are going to awaken and that you will wake refreshed and revitalised. Then you make it happen.

Lastly, we can practice relaxation and the preparations for Dream Yoga.

Dreaming

Ken Wilber, who is one of my heroes, wrote the following pieces on the constancy of consciousness through all of the states of mind, waking, sleeping and dreaming in his book One Taste.

"This constant consciousness through all states - waking, dreaming, and sleeping - tends to occur after many years of meditating; in my case, about twenty-five years. The signs are very simple: you are conscious in the waking state, and then, as you fall asleep and start to dream, you still remain conscious of the dreaming"

"Then as you pass into deep, dreamless sleep, you still remain conscious, but now you are aware of nothing but vast pure emptiness, with no content whatsoever. But "aware of

" is not quite right, since there is no duality here. It's more like, there is simply pure consciousness itself, without qualities or contents or subjects of objects, a vast pure emptiness that is not nothing but is still unqualifiable"

"Then as you come out of the deep sleep state, you see the mind and the dream state arise and take form. That is, out of causal emptiness there arises the subtle mind (dreams, images, symbols, concepts, visions, forms), and you witness this emergence. The dream state continues for a while, and then, as you begin to wake up, you can see the entire gross realm, the physical realm - your body, the bed, the room, the physical universe, nature - arise directly out of the subtle mind state".

This is the constancy of consciousness through all three dimensions of consciousness, the final recognition being that all the states are one flow with transcendental consciousness. All of the possibilities of pure emptiness are utterly inseparable with the movement and play of form.
So, which part of our sleep cycle do dreams happen in again?

Dreams occur in REM sleep and involve visual and hallucinatory elements. Such dreams will often use any and all of the senses.
But why do we dream?

Dreaming appears to function in a variety of ways. The first thing that is clear from scientific studies is that both REM and NREM sleep are crucial for mental wellbeing. The integrity of waking consciousness really does depend on the integrity of both sleep and dream consciousness, and getting enough sleep and dreaming sufficiently does appear to be crucial for human wellbeing.
Dreams can also highlight what we are not paying attention to. Dreams can bring to our awareness issues that we may do well to start looking at. One reason that people keep dream journals is that when issues are brought to mind (literally), one can then choose to engage with those issues during waking consciousness.

One may well choose to do this with the help of a competent teacher or therapist. If you choose to go for it alone, which is possible, then you need really good awareness and resolution skills, and probably some very good friends.

We also dream about what we spend most of our time thinking about and paying attention to.

What do you spend your time thinking about, paying attention to, and doing?

An established sitting practice will also help bring into view what sort of cerebral activity your brain gets up to. Remember, brains do cerebral activity, thats what they are partly for.

As long as you don't criminalise your thinking and drive it into the shadows, or identify with it and believe it is who you are, that you are this cerebral process, or act mindlessly based on this, then there is no problem with any thought process.

We may well dream about recent memories that are emotionally charged, dreams really can help in emotional processing.

We may dream about any activity or event that is temporally recent to our sleep time.

What were you doing just before bedtime?

You could also dream about any other historical memories that have not been effectively processed. The dreams here will bear some resemblance with the event.

Dreams also function to consolidate memories and to regulate and integrate emotions, particularly the more complex and difficult ones that we struggle with. In this way, dreams can help facilitate emotional homeostasis. Dreams help us integrate and make emotional sense of our life experience and its challenges.

Dreams can also act, as our thinking often does, as a form of pre-emptive threat rehearsal.

How often do you have apprehensive thoughts about what may happen in the future?

Well dreams also serve us in this area. We commonly do mental rehearsal in our minds about potential social interactions we are worried about. Some solution focused therapies utilise this apprehensive capacity for performance perfection and generation of social ease. Dreams can help in a similar way.

Dreams also help rewire neurology, building new synaptic connections, in the light of experience. Our synaptic web is constantly undergoing changes in the light of experience, this is the very basis of neuroplasticity. Dreams, along with meditation, somatic practice, and a whole variety of therapeutic practices, offer the opportunity for rewiring the brain.

So, REM dreams are complex, visual and hallucinatory and their function appears to include all of the above.

REM sleep is also theorised to be prior to waking consciousness. This is evidenced by the occurrence of dreams in the foetus in the womb. Alan Hobson who came up with this theory suggests that REM sleep is also in the service of developing brain function, brain function that will eventually lead to waking consciousness.

Dreaming is a relatively recent evolutionary development requiring a link between the cortex and the thalamus in the brain. The cortex processes sensation, thought and meaning, and the thalamus works as an informational relay between sensation, motor function, memory, wakefulness and sleeping, amongst other things. This link is called the cortico-thalamic-cortico loop (CTC loop). No CTC loop equals no dreams.

Lucid dreaming

Lucid dreams are simply dreams in which you are aware that you are dreaming. Lucid dreamers can cultivate varying levels of control over their dream states. This lucidity and control are probably achieved by switching on parts of the left pre-frontal cortex and another part of the brain, the precuneus, whilst keeping all other aspects of the body that relate to waking consciousness switched off.

Lucid dreamers score more highly on questions relating to self-confi dence, tend to be more assertive, and show a greater sense of satisfaction, direction and clarity with their life. Lucid dreamers also report they are relatively free of mental health problems compared to non-lucid dreamers. Lucid dreamers may well process difficult emotions and trauma more rapidly than non-lucid dreamers. Lucid dreamers have been shown to experience lower levels of stress than non-lucid dreamers in traumatic situations, such as war zones, due to their capacity to be in command of their minds processing more effectively.

Being in command of dreams may also open one to accelerated learning. People who perform tasks in their dreams have been evidenced to be better at performing the same tasks the next day. This is because the neural networks involved in both real and imagined tasks and movements are very similar. Training these areas through visualisation and Dream Yoga can facilitate enhanced performance in waking life. Research supports the theory that neural networks involved in imagined tasks and lucid dreaming are the same. The benefit from lucid dreaming could be even greater than in visualisation practices because of the greater feeling of reality in lucid dreaming. This feeling is enhanced by the emotional content of lucid dreaming, which is usually less present in visualisation. Such lucid dreaming will boost the learning process.

Dream Yoga

Practising Dream Yoga is a profound way to deepen somatic practices and meditation. Dream Yoga can be used as a method in conjunction with meditation. Dream Yoga can be used to enhance any skill, and yet can also be much deeper than this as it extends awareness through the dream dimension into deep sleep itself. To do this, a high level of witness consciousness is needed.

Dream Yoga, as opposed to Lucid dreaming, is much more about cultivating constant witnessing consciousness. It is carrying the meditative process into the dream dimension.

In Dream Yoga there is less desire to fly, have orgies, eat great food and so on. In both Dream Yoga and meditation the intention is to find that which underlies experience, not simply have more and more exotic experiences.

Dream Yoga allows one to apprehend the nature of subjective reality through the acceleration of interiorisation. When we also realise that dream reality is controllable, and similar to waking reality, we can begin to understand the role of awareness in waking, dreaming and potentially deep sleep and enlightened states of super-clarity.

Beginning Dream Yoga

Taking time during waking consciousness to study your palm is a good method to begin the practice of Dream Yoga. Study it well enough so you can call it up in your mind. Get to know its shape, its wrinkles, its idiosyncrasies and characteristics. Gaze at your palm, study it at random moments through the course of the day and get to know it well.

This simple method builds on the development of palm awareness. The practice of lucid dreaming then follows these eight stages.

- Observe the palm of the hand before sleeping and decide to wake up in the dream.

- Now notice that you are dreaming.

- You will notice it, you will feel it because of the slightly unusual play of the senses or movement back and forth in time. The laws of physics may well be being transcended.

- When you first realise that you are dreaming then immediately raise your palm to your face and look at it.

- See your palm in the dream, when you hold it to your face you will know you are dreaming.

- Once you know you are dreaming you can begin to learn to control the dream.

- Through practice you learn to control the dream, resolve arising unconscious material or practice skills you want to learn and deepen in awareness.

- Wake up and remember your dream and integrate waking and dreaming consciousness.

The Nine Steps of Dream Yoga

This is the means to extend lucid dreaming into the path of awakening.

- First, we have to realise that we are dreaming, we have to become lucid.

- Next, to become steady and effortless in the presence of awareness in the dream. Sustain lucidity with ease.

- The third step is to work with transforming the dream and become skilful at this.

- Fourth, is to recognise all appearances as being empty of any inher ence. Here, we know that all flows of form have no solidity, no defini tion of their own, no permanence, and are all products and projections of mind. They are all, in essence, illusory.

- The fifth step is to come to stable, expansive, luminous awareness. This is the practice of no control. Here we simply witness, we observe all arising phenomena. We witness and remain totally uninvolved, and deepen into this witness state, this observing self, until it be comes effortless.

- Sixth, is to allow the witness, the observing self, to dissolve. The dream flow can now unify with the clear light of awareness. this unicity previously disguised by the witness, becomes self-evident.

- In the seventh step, we recognise in the dream state that form and emptiness are inseparable, one flow. These seven phases of practice also now flow into one another.

- Eighth, what can now arise is that luminous awareness begins to osmotically leak into the deep sleep state and, as mentioned in the Ken Wilber quote, deep sleep states also become known as luminous awareness or luminous-clarity.

- The ninth and final step is understanding the essence of deep sleep as luminosity, cognisant, aware and perfect. This is then known as not different from one's awareness in meditative equipoise, which one also practices in the waking state.

Dream Yoga is traditionally practiced in conjunction with a meditation practice.

Now, before going to sleep
Consider your day.

What happened?

How did you respond to what happened?

What would you have done differently?

What would you have done the same?

What have you learned about love, life and your self?

What golden moments were there to totally celebrate?

How will you cherish them?

Now, tune into your breath, let go of the day and study your dominant hand.
Study your hand well and decide to wake up in your dreams. When waking up in your dreams play freely and then choose to look at the mind that is dreaming.
Choose to rest well, dream lucidly and well, and to wake up feeling refreshed, rejuvenated and ready for the next day of creative empowerment.

micropractices - mindfulness moments

Remember, practice is intended to bear fruit. Feeling good is great, practising is cool and it can be fun, however, practice is meant to free the practitioner from the great illusion. The great illusion is that we are a subject, a doer, a separate being, separate from the world around us, from each other and from the interdependent matrix of the cosmos.

Living as a separate self-sense is ultimately unsatisfactory, sooner or later, even in the land of plenty, this separateness leads to inherent tension suffering within this position. The opposite of suffering is joy, relaxation, ease, happiness, wellbeing and real peace. We practice to find these qualities in our lives.
A method to allow the flow of more awakened qualities through daily life is to pay attention to what is actually happening in each moment. This paying attention in each moment, or mindfulness, can have a

focus to it.
What do we pay attention to?

It can be anything that's happening. Yet there are key events and experiences available to us that really allow and invite the mind to settle, relax and drop into presence. When we pay attention to a particular event or experience with such attention this can be used as a micro-practice. A micro-practice is a brief and informal practice of mindful attention.

Micro-practices are simply moments of mindfulness, clarity and presence in daily life. Mindfulness as it is taught in workspaces around the world is one of these approaches to practice. Mindfulness is the practice of choice if you fail to be present. If you are feeling stressed, then practice mindfulness to delimit or prevent stress.

Beyond mindfulness is realisation, pure presence-being. Presence-being is the outcome of meditation practice. In presence-being, mindfulness arises without effort, a natural result of presence.
Whether you are changing a baby's nappy, cooking a meal, sorting your accounts, working on a computer or shopping, every moment is available for mindfulness, deeper presence, deeper awareness, greater clarity, compassion and true engagement. These moments of possibility are micro-practices.
Presence and awareness become a normal part of life as clarity arises and begins to flow in streams. The pouring of precious life-energy into the self- story, its narratives and self-orientation then gradually diminish. The meanings about the world it makes up, slowly lose their power and become transparent. Transparency of our egoic motivations and drives is conscious co-evolution.

- Micro-practices are opportunities for presence and engagement.

- Micro-practices are methods of carrying the depth, insight and pres ence of formal practice into daily life.

- Micro-practices encourage moments of clarity leading to a stream of clarity which becomes the ever present theme of daily life.

- Micro-practices are a method of expanding compassion, weaving it through every flavour and nuance of daily life.

Two forms of stress and the self-sense

The sense-of-self, commonly called ego, creates relentless narratives and meaning-making, known to us all as monkey mind, is a head full of thoughts. We may be planning, analysing, scheming or working out what might be the best future possibilities for our business. Meditation calms the mind and helps us see our patterns clearly so we don't get caught up in them. Daily life commonly reinforces these patterns through its relentless demands and stresses.

Stress as we experience it, is largely a function of the sense-of-self. We can think of stress as two forms.

The first is environmental stress

Environmental stress includes temperature, sound, dehydration, starvation, poor air quality, and lack of sleep. Here the environmental conditions need to be changed so that one can get out of survival mode. Actualisation, realisation is harder when we are in survival mode.

The second is perceptual stress

Perceptual stress is a function of the appearance of two. This means there has to be a subject (I) in relationship to objects (thoughts, feelings, things and you) and stress appears out of this dynamic. Our 'sense-of-self' is the subject that creates a perception of threat. The perception of threat and our response to that leads to our experience of stress and to the stress response.

Daily life offers profound opportunities to notice how we fabricate our sense-of-self, how we generate perceptions of threat and build neuro-muscular stories of separation and thus stress from this. These neuromuscular tensions are the ones we seek to undo in somatic practices, meditation and through mindfulness based stress reduction.

Somatic methods of practice can help resolve the contractions of stress, they are also ideally a method of preventing them occurring in the first place. This comes from embodied awareness, where we can catch the patterns as they arise and then rapidly drop them.

Micro-practices are a method of expanding compassion and clarity, weaving it through every flavour and nuance of daily life. Whether you are changing a baby's nappy, cooking a meal, sorting your accounts or shopping, every moment is available for deeper presence, deeper awareness, greater clarity, more love, and true engagement.

As presence and awareness become a normal part of everyday life, as clarity arises and begins to flow in streams of engaged presence, then the pouring of precious life-energy into the self-story diminishes and this fabrication slowly loses its power, loses its grip and becomes transparent.

The transparent self-story and self-sense has utilitarian value, it allows one to move and act in the world. The source of action is now presence, pure awareness and this now radiates out into the world through the self-construct which has been assigned it's rightful place as servant of awareness.

breathing breaks - central nervous system (CNS) management

Take breathing breaks at least four times a day, go on, take nine full deep breaths each time, thoroughly enjoy them, fully feel them. Be at peace.
Simple micro-practices like this keep the CNS in relaxation mode as much as possible, and allow a more loving and engaged perspective on life.
Many of us have stressful jobs, busy lives, and relentless demands for our time, attention, and money. The informational demands of modern life with all of our technological communication is phenomenal. To simply survive the manifold commands of everyday life in the contemporary world we need good CNS management skills. Taking responsibility for one's own CNS and keeping it as relaxed and responsive as possible, rather than reactive, is a good counterpoint to these relentless adrenalised and insistent requirements of contemporary life.

Stress is known to contribute to all the major killers including the cardio-vascular diseases (strokes and heart attacks), diabetes, and cancer. Stress is implicated in many other conditions from eczema to asthma, headaches to heartburn and arthritis to early onset conditions of ageing. Stress is a killer that can also debilitate your health, consume your wealth and destroy the quality of your life and the lives of those around you.

Having potent tools like somatic practice, relaxation skills, meditation and mindfulness in our toolbox, we can learn to cultivate a nervous system that rests more easily in, what Herbert Benson called, the Relaxation Response. The alternative is living in, what Hans Selye called, the Stress Response, or as some call it the Physical Emergency Response (PER). Living in the PER leads to less effective neurological function, reduced immunity and potentially reduced longevity.
Why live this when alternatives are available?

It is better to work with prevention than cure. Begin your practices now, use mindfulness, meditation, relaxation, yoga-asana and all the practices of conscious co-evolution and begin now, literally save your own life.
All of life is an opportunity for practice, realisation and resilient joy. When each one of us takes responsibility for our own thinking, our own feelings, our own behaviour, and all the consequences of these, we have a conscious culture. These are the requirements of conscious co-evolution, responsibility for all of our own thinking, feeling and behaving and all their consequences.

The antithesis of such a world is a culture of shame, blame, guilt, comparison and complaining. When we blame everyone else for our reality and refuse to take responsibility then we have a culture of blame. Living from a place of reaction, reflexive patterning, unconsciousness, and minimal choice is the way of disempowerment.
Shame is toxic and best avoided, it creates lack of worth and low esteem.
Comparison is the thief of joy and love.
Guilt is useful in small doses to facilitate learning and after that is toxic or addictive, creating martyr states.
Complaint is simply not taking responsibility, if you don't like something then start doing something about it, that is my recommendation. From now on, choose to take responsibility.
Blame puts you in the place of the victim, whilst responsibility is empowering.

Taking control of our own CNS and enable internal creative space, between stimulus and response. This is the way of choice, consciousness, awareness, responsibility and conscious co-evolution.

To create a conscious culture we have to be conscious and aware. A culture is made of individuals. If, we, as individuals are less than conscious, living in reflexive patterns, disempowered and blaming then that is the essence of our culture.
If, we, as individuals within the culture are taking responsibility for our own CNS, our own thinking, our own feelings, our own behaviour, and living from a place of spacious creativity then that is the essence of our culture.

Breathwork, along with a good somatic practice, meditation and understanding how our own brain works is the most rapid route to work directly with our own CNS. Take regular breathing breaks, it works.

relational practice - biophilia plus

We are relationship. We are spiralling DNA contributed from our parents. We are flesh made of our mothers breast milk. We are flesh made of sunlight, water and minerals from plants and the soil. We are air. We are vortices of vibrating particles temporarily woven together into the appearance of a separate life-form. We are the learnt emotions from our families and cultures. However our families interpreted and communicated the body-based sensations that we call emotions and feelings, we learn relationally.
Our concepts, ideas, political views, philosophies, values and beliefs we learn relationally.
There is not one part of us that is not relationship.
This is why relational depth in psychotherapy works. it gives us closeness, trust, reflection and assisted witness consciousness for us to make the neurological changes we then choose and probably need to make. This makes our experience of life relationally richer.

We need people. We need touch and hugs to be well and happy. Virgina Satir, the great family therapist reckoned we needed upwards of a dozen hugs a day to be relationally rich.

With our vulnerable central surface facing the world we benefit from ventral surface to ventral surface contact, it helps us put up less emotional armour or take down our emotional armour. People with deeply embedded emotional armour struggle to be close to others, they may have accumulated money and dominance (different to power) however they are relationally poor.

All the art forms of conscious co-evolution if you look at them are relational work. From communication, community, self-reflective consciousness, celebration and conflict-resolution through understanding our relationship with our commensals and symbionts and conservation of diversity, all are aspects of our relational work.

When we understand we are relationship, that relationship and communication and community is always what is happening then we have no choice but to work on the quality of these.
Appreciation of and devotion to the essence, diversity and quality of life is Biophilia. Practicing bio-philia celebrates life. We can find gratitude and devotion for all of life bubbling through our heart-space, after all we are this.

Lets have a quick look at worship as a form of changing our relational stance. People worship and bow to whatever they perceive is greater than their own limited body-mind feeling of separation.
People supplicate and wish for things to be different than they are.
What do people worship?

Some worship their ishta-devata, a chosen deity form, their personal avenue to transcendence of the personal to the transpersonal.
Some worship an uncultured deity form, what their culture convinced them they should believe in, sometimes at pain of death.
Some worship the infinite and all pervasive formlessness of the absolute.
Some worship the sacred essence of life.
Some worship the awesome vastness of the universe and beyond.
Some worship their teacher, their Guru.
Some worship their consort-lover as the essence of the divine.
Some worship nothing, void.
Some worship the dark side or power and control.

Some bow to science and empirical method.
Many people bow in worship unconsciously…
People commonly bow to some limited principle or pseudo-deity. Usually the pseudo-deity is fear, money, power, sexual charisma, eroticism, superficial beauty (symmetry and surfaces), cultural pressure, group membership, youth or status.

Whatever relational approach you utilise, to experience yourself in relationship to the totality and the transpersonal (which you already are) you have to believe it enough to make it work. You have to enjoy it enough to do it often, and it has to cultivate sufficient neuro-chemicals of bliss for you to change perspective.

Belief is relational medicine if it is held gently and used with flexibility. Rigid belief is imprisonment and relational destruction.

Understanding belief as medicine is an evolutionary stance, one that requires courage, wisdom, intelligence and clarity of mind. Realise that devotion is one way to take you out of your self into the no-Self, from the personal to the transpersonal. The exploration, inquiry or dance between personal and transpersonal is a relational one.
What are the qualities of the experience of the transpersonal?

Qualities of the transpersonal

We go beyond the separate experience of self to the transpersonal experience and vision of no-Self.

We enter into timelessness. This manifests as time slowing or stopping, as an experience of infinity or the expanse of time or ultimately as that which transcends the very experience of time.

We enter into spacelessness. The experience of being space first, beyond separation and solidity and then finding a quality which is beyond the movement and vibration of space-time. This inner quality is called emptiness, formlessness and so on.

Effortlessness. There is no effort needed to achieve this state and no effort to be done. This is called Sahaja in Sanskrit and is called Grace in other traditions.

Real wealth. The richness and wealth of the experience transcends all visions of wealth, the pointless futility of profit and empire (and golden towers) becomes fully apparent.

Clarity. The wisdom arising as we understand the experience of being a separate life-form from the perspective of vastness alters everything. We can no longer inhabit the desires and obsessions of separation in the same old way. Everything changes, there is a turning about in the seat of consciousness and life becomes service to the unicity.

Compassion. The naturally arising feeling state of vastness and the clarity that comes with this is compassion. We get how it is to feel solid and real, we know how it is to feel separate. We see the obsessive nature and pointlessness of achievement and success, and yet we also see and know how activity and the fruits of activity can be functional to make this world a better place for all.

Deathlessness. We experience a continuity of consciousness, a place in us which is all life, all lives. This brings us home to the real, to the knowing of a place in us that no longer fears death and sees it as a transition.

This is the experience of the transpersonal that arises through the inner work.

Through bio-philiac devotion we can begin to cultivate the neurology of wonder, deep love and connection. Biophilia naturally generates these qualities, all you have to do is open your eyes, your mind and your heart to the amazing miracle of life. In this space of wonder, appreciation, gratitude and connection generated by this practice, the practitioner may begin to see the truth of their deeper nature beyond the limited self-construct. Then, through surrender to this greater whole, one begins to experience living scintillating truth beyond the ego and slowly becomes this greater transpersonal possibility.

If we create a spectrum of devotion with whatever our belief represents as being the apogee of affection, devotion and truth then we use the walls of the 'pit of duality' or separate self and other, to pull ourselves out into unicity. From the experience of fearful separateness we use our psychological projections through belief to lift our thinking, feeling and visioning to bring us closer to the state of unicity that is always, already present. We simply fail to see it normally so we use belief to remind us…

Yes life is miraculous, amazing, paradoxical, beyond the understanding of our minds.

- Devotion can be a naturally arising sense of pure gratitude for every aris ing moment, no matter what is happening.
- In fact, from the view of non-dual realisation, devotion is a natural out come. From the view of separation, devotion is a practice.

In the beginning, for those of us contemporary beings caught up with consumption and instant gratification, conscious devotion can be uncomfortable, even impossible. However babies, puppies, wild nature and other moments of beauty open the hearts of some. Suffering and pain opens the hearts of others. If nothing else works then, as you die, you will open. Either way, the heart will open.

The practices of devotion are methods for opening the heart during life, and through this the appreciative mind. Devotion, celebration, and gratitude go hand in hand. This trio support each other and assist the heart to open.

Celebration can be practised individually or collectively. Collective celebrations, whether ceremonial or spontaneous, bring communities of practitioners into a deeper synergy and engagement. I for one love ceremony, ceremony crafted by those who attend. There may be a focus and a facilitator, but the ritual itself is not ossified by convention but free to arise in the immediacy of the embrace of community. Such celebration can require a certain openness and ease though, this may have to be cultivated through the other practices mentioned in this and other sections of this book.

Why not be devoted to love in all its dances, devoted to wisdom and truth, fully devoted to the deepest freedom for all beings everywhere?

How about being a devotee of conscious co-evolution, a bio-philiac?

We are relational beings. We are never not in relationship. Growing and nourishing our mutual relationships is the work of conscious, aware co-evolution.

Seeing others through the eyes of love

People often act out of fear, unconscious programming, and distorted views.

From feeling like a self-sense which is isolated and different to the rest of the universe, the root feeling that arises is fear, or even unmitigated terror.

This separateness results in the patterns and emotions that include fear, hatred, anger, jealousy, envy, blame, shame, and toxic guilt.

For sure, we mostly live from our patterns and carry out behaviours that increase the collective burden of suffering and pain.

Yet, the vision of conscious co-evolution is that underneath all of this, every single being is a 'Buddha to be', awakened pure awareness. Inside the most nefarious, stupid and vile acts, somewhere deep inside is a 'Buddha to be' wrapped in twisted sheaths of distorted separation, fear and pain.

Maybe your enlightened expectation, your realisation of love and wisdom in the core of all beings will help bring this out in them, and in your self?

Above all else this is a relational practice, because when we insist on seeing the most vibrant possibilities in others, it is more likely this will happen. Lets see each other through the eyes of love, let us invite each other into transparency and transpersonal wholeness.

ecological awareness - rewilding...

We are ecology. The foolish illusion cultivated by centuries of belief that we are separate and superior to our planet has led to untold devastation to our planetary home.

Whilst Elon Musk may have visions of human habitation beyond Mars, we are far from this. We live on one planet, this is it. We are totally interdependent with myriads of other lifeform on this planet as we will find out ion we keep pushing the boundaries of extinction. We will find that we are part of a web, not some independent controller.

People suffer from nature deficit disorder. People suffer from the illusion of separation and live in some virtual fantasy realm or ivory towers of privilege and plenty.

Coming back to earth is a powerful experience of reintegration. I would invite all CEO's of big corporations and banks and help them to rewild if they would come. I'm not talking about going out on the golf course or for a weekends fishing. Im talking about getting naked and cold, hungry and thirsty. I'm talking about learning how to make fire, how to find clean drinking water and how to live in harmony with our planet instead of seeking to dominate it. There is no wilderness anywhere except in the human mind and in human cities. The view of the wildness of nature is because we no longer have a healthy relationship with the life-form, landscape and elements.

Rewilding takes us back into wild nature and helps us remember what is valuable and precious here on planet earth. Rewilding helps us cultivate a healthy relationship with ourselves, with other life-form and the land and the elements.

diet - an intimate relationship to life-form

Your body knows what it needs to eat. If you listen carefully it will tell you, it really will.

- Don't eat to cover feelings or to find comfort, look at the feelings and resolve them

- Don't eat because it's there, this is not a healthy relationship with food or yourself

- Don't eat because it's mealtime, you're not an eating machine. Some people need regular meals, others do better eating less often, some do better grazing through the day.
  What eating style works best for you?

  How do you know?

- Don't eat because others are eating, sometimes this is okay, but to make a regular habit of it is a real problem. We humans use eating as a celebration, of course this comes from our hunter gatherer and agrarian ancestry. We still celebrate with food, but to ignore your body needs completely is a way to begin losing the capacity to listen to what your needs really are.

- Don't eat because your diet says you have to, this is not listening to your body but imposing an idea on your body. Whilst diets may serve some to find more balance with eating, longer term I would recommend listening more to what you body is asking for.

- Eat mostly because you're hungry and your body needs it.

I find it good to fast for short periods, I'm not a fan of long fasts, no more than three days for me and nowadays, only when I can relax into the fast. I don't like long fasts with a busy and demanding life. Each to their own, however I find short fasts work better for me. I wait to eat each day until I am hungry, Again this doesn't work for everybody, some people need breakfast first thing, I simply cant eat in the mornings. People are different.
What works for you?

For a body to digest food the nervous system has to be in relaxation response, parasympathetic. If your autonomic nervous system (ANS) is in stress response-activity mode then blood flows away from the digestive system and effective digestion and absorption of what you put in your belly is not possible. Only if your autonomic nervous system (ANS) is in relaxation response with blood flowing to your intestines can effective absorption happen. The ANS is the part that runs all the unseen, unconscious processes in your body including digestion. The two branches of the ANS are the stress response - activity mode (fight, flight, fright and freeze) and the relaxation response (rest and digest). In the stress response blood flows away from the digestive system to the muscles and brain. Only in the relaxation response does blood flow to the intestines and facilitate effective digestion. It is important to be relaxed before, during and after you eat. If you don't relax before, during and after you eat, then the food will pass through your intestines poorly digested and possibly irritate your bowels. You certainly wont get as much benefit as you could from eating it and this is a waste of your energy, a waste of food and a waste of the lifeform you have consumed.

Arguably you might as well throw the plate of food straight down the toilet and save your body the energy of pushing tit through the intestines and only partially digesting it.
Consider it a practice of wellbeing to take a couple of minutes to relax before you eat, to take your time eating and to relax afterwards then you are on track to using food wisely.

I have come across estimates of some ninety percent of women and increasing numbers of men having food related issues. This means that before they eat, people with food related issues consider wether the food they eat will affect their weight, their shape or what they look like in someone else's eyes.
This is a criminal waste of life energy and creativity. All those women and men who are suffering from feelings of inadequacy, un-love and low self-esteem who then worry about whether they will be lovable if they eat or don't eat a particular food could, instead, be contributing to the collective of humanity with their creative powers. These creative powers are being used up in worrying about consuming another x calories or not. This is a symptom of an imbalanced culture, a culture of surfaces and superficiality where body shape is clearly more important than creative power, personality or capacity to love or be loved for who we are.
Let's free ourselves and future generations from such facile nonsense and end the promotion of inadequacy, your too thin, too fat, too small, too large, too this or that… a promotion that leads people to believe they are unlovable and inadequate.

Eating well is necessary for survival and to be well. Again many people are obsessed with healthy diets. They are obsessed to the degree they would happily kill the planet with dietary air miles rather than let go of any food related neurosis. No one is going to become immortal from eating more of a particular vitamin or mineral. Every one who eats is going to die, sooner or later. Eating sensibly and well and being obsessed by food are two different things.
Remember good health is just a slower way to die!

Below are a few eating practices.
Whenever you eat, take time to relax beforehand, even a couple of minutes. Relax and take your time as you eat and try to relax afterwards for

half an hour. If you don't, your not doing yourself any favours, you are making yourself less efficient and promoting ill health.
Now, make your food beautiful. Have a visual feast too.
Totally enjoy the smell and fragrance.
What does the aroma communicate?

Whenever you eat enjoy the taste, really enjoy it!
If you can, eat with your fingers so you involve the sense of touch too, feel your food.
How is this?

Getting all the senses involved gives you a sensual and sensory relationship with your food. Knives and forks distance you from the food.
Love your food.
Offer gratitude to the interdependent web each time you eat.
Best not to eat highly processed commercialised food, it's not really food. Best eat organic, because, if grown well, it can be kinder to our environment and our bodies, and they are not separate are they?
Organic pricing can be prohibitive though for poorer people. What can we do to help with this?

Let's pay attention to air miles until we get some seriously carbon-neutral green aviation fuel. We have the technology for this and prototype green plans have been tested and they work. What we lack is political will and investment, as usual.
Will you choose to purchase out of season fruits and vegetables shipped for miles around the planet with the idea that it's good for you?

Will you choose to eat energy expensive beef, when that prime arable land could be used for other crops?

Will you choose to eat animals tortured in cramped conditions, unable to move properly and then slaughtered and butchered in death factories?

If it's not good for the planet can it really be good for you?

This may mean we have to pay attention more to what grows on our own land, in our own neighbourhood. Is this possible?

What's stopping us from doing this?

What changes do you have to make to your diet to facilitate a carbon neutral diet?

- A challenge for all vegans and vegetarians - eat only what grows within a thirty kilometre radius from your home.

- A challenge for all meat eaters - kill, gut, skin and butcher the animal you are wanting to eat. Make sure it ran around freely before you do this. If you can't do this maybe don't eat it!

Food is medicine!

Depending on your context, climate, condition, cultural history and constitution maybe you will require different or specific foods.
Many people will try to tell you what you need to be eating and why. Hopefully I am not doing that, hopefully I am stimulating inquiry to stay open to possibilities, I don't believe there are easy answers here. Many people will come up with convincing grand narratives to justify their beliefs, I won't do that. I feel the only grand narrative we need to be paying attention to at the moment is animal welfare and ecological issues.
You're going to have to work out your answers yourself through inquiry, study of your own system and what you can find out about ecological costs of the foodstuff you eat. The whole point of a pragmatic ethical practice and inquiry is to engage openly and honestly in dialogue and mutual empowerment, not simply to follow an 'off the shelf belief system' with easy answers.
How about the idea that no one diet fits all?

You're going to have to listen to inner feedback and work with your relationship to the environment as well as within any social context you inhabit.
What medicine do you need?

What intimate dietary relationship do you have with the environment?

So please celebrate and enjoy food and keep checking in with the carbon inquiry and the ethics of diet.

Remember, eating is interaction, it is relationship, it is conscious co-evolution.

Matrix Meditation of Conscious Co-Evolution

And now reflect on…

This beautifully complex web of interaction, inter-dependence and co-evolutionary arising. Reflect on the endless web of cause and effect. Reflect on the endless web of co-evolution and begin to see your own life through this lens of inter connection.

Feeling and knowing this profound sense of connectedness, meditate on your body. Be aware of every part, scan it from top to bottom and back again until you can hold all of it appreciatively in your awareness field.
Be aware of how your body is a part of a much bigger whole, your local ecology and the planet.

Be aware of all of this as 'in flow'. Being aware of this form as flowing process resting in the temporary cohesion of 'your body' before returning your attention to the larger flow of ecology.
Be aware of every complex web of relationship that has led to your existence and which continues to allow you to exist. Go deep in this.

Recognise and realise everything in your life and all life as a continuously connected stream, one seamless flow.

Now reflect on your emotional world and feel all the complex influences, positive and negative, that have helped form your emotional view of reality. Reflect on your capacity for emotional intelligence and the resolution of all emotions from expression of duality into expressions of unicity, the one as the many and the many as the one.

See and feel your cognitive realm and recognise some of the vast input from the minds of so many Beings, past and present, that allow you to construct the ways you think, the meanings you make and the stories you tell about your self and your world. Find gratitude and appreciation.

Explore this engaged, process-meditation in daily life.
Reflect as you take food and drink.
Reflect on systemic interdependence as you excrete.
Be aware as you move, behave and relate in the world.
Remember and be aware that you are never not in relationship.
As you feel and think be aware of the vast complexity of inter-connection that allows you to be who you are.
Relax into it, have fun with it and participate well in the matrix of existence.

Arrive, in your own time, at a profoundly deep and joyful sense of gratitude for this life that flows through you and through all beings and live powerfully from this place.

The Outer Work

We've had a look at many aspects of the outer work already.
We have to rethink everything, redream everything, sift the baby from the bathwater of the past and recreate a conscious culture, this is the essential message of conscious co-evolution.
This is becoming increasingly clear as carbon dioxide levels rise, the highest for eight hundred thousand years, the ice melts and the dinosaurs of consumption oriented capitalism seek to continue business as usual.
The global economy is also collapsing and we the people are still paying as we bail out banks and bankers, we are still paying their taxes to cover the loss.

We've also looked at what an intelligent childcare and education system might comprise and the crucial importance of this. We've considered conflict and conflict resolution and many other facets of what being a contemporary human is like, what to pay attention to and how to begin to grow a conscious culture that stewards our planetary home.
Yes eveything needs to be rethought.

One of the big elements from yogic culture that I like and feel is important is ethical livelihood. We've not looked at this really, so here are a few questions to get the ball rolling.
What do you do to generate your income?

What is the relationship between your income generation and your environmental and social ethics?

How does the creation of your income affect other people?

Does the production of your income require other people or other lifeforms to suffer?

Right livelihood matters especially if we seek to pay skilful attention to the consequences of all our actions whilst sustaining joy, fun, beauty and love in our lives.
This is, and always has been, a tightrope walk that requires considera-

tion, patience, and the capacity to work with paradox.

We can ask ourselves how our actions in the world create greater joy and openness for ourselves and all other beings. These kinds of worthy inquiry are a part of our work, a part that really facilitates the movement of pristine awareness into everyday life.

How does your working life support your practice and your evolution into awakening?

Are you following your calling with your work life, is it your purpose, or just a way of making a living?

What is purpose?

Is purpose something you craft?

I like to think of purpose as a heartfelt feeling of aptness, as something we craft and evolve through the course of our lives. I think of purpose as a flow of direction, a navigator principle rather than a goal.

For me the subtle qualities of purpose can flex and change but the overall sense of direction remains.

Is that how it is for you?

If it is different, how is it different?

What are you willing to do to follow your purpose, to move with your calling?

How will you make a good living whilst following your deepest hearts calling?

What are the costs to your sense of joy and wellbeing if you sacrifice your deepest calling at the shrine of convenience, profit and convention?

There may be no getting it 'right'. There will probably always be attention needed to facilitate the balance of right livelihood and income generation. There may always be new energies to move with and new concerns to pay attention to. Each new challenge will certainly offer its opportunities for growth though.

How will you stay open, loving and joyful amidst the clash and thun-

der of conflict, chaos, collapse, and reconstruction?

How might you best rise to the challenges of change and growth?

consumption

People often buy consumer items in an endeavour to feel secure, in control, approved of, loved, connected, and having an identity, being someone. This endeavour may be conscious or unconscious. This kind of consumerism is relentless because it never works more than temporarily. It is like sticking band-aids on a major haemorrhage. It is looking for love, security, truth, unicity, and identity in all the wrong places. If the places we look for these qualities are all impermanent, the result will be impermanent. This is why we do the inner work.
Consumer goods are superbly impermanent, even the best of them. The worst of them are almost instant landfill.

The consequences of 'not having' on this planet include hunger, thirst, homelessness, and destitution. The global economic system appears to control the 'have nots' through fear, debt and servitude.
If we are seeking to step from ignorance to consciousness, from reflexive habits to authentic freedom, and from feudal servitude to collective freedom, then what and how will we be consuming?

It is worth understanding that 'buying' simply means accessing resources. We are seeking to access resources which we are using for the greatest good of all, buying 'stuff' is legitimate. We need access to resources.

If we buy (access) what we really need, what we really want, what serves our growth and through this the greater good, this then leads us to authentic freedom, individually and collectively.
Recognising the wealth we receive daily and celebrating the abundance of this universe we can choose to cultivate the attitude of gratitude at every opportunity, until it becomes a way of life.

Money gives us three things...
- Access to resources
- Space for choice
- Something we exchange our life energy for and use as a token of trade

The other things that money gives, such as feelings of possession, security, status and identity are all low-level ego desires, temporary states that serve only the cause of deeper separation and human suffering. There is nothing wrong with being ethically wealthy and using wealth for the cause of conscious, aware co-evolution and authentic freedom. ***The question is, are you awake enough, wise enough, loving enough not to be seduced by the power that wealth can confer?***

I trust so... I am and it really is no big deal.
We see so many folk in the media who fail at managing their greed and hunger for power that we almost take it for granted that wealth will corrupt. Not if your really into conscious co-evolution. In that case resource use is simply another tool to help build an even more amazing world.

As the cost of extracting oil and other strategic resources from the earth rises, as the cost of energy and production thereby rises, then recycling everything is worthwhile at last, and we can no longer buy into the myth of infinite and relentless growth.
This planet really does have limits to growth. Limits to growth means that an economic system based on the infinitely expanding production of consumer goods is unsustainable. If we don't pay attention to the balance, the homoeostasis needed, then the system crashes into unsustainability.
The enlightened choice is to live, buy, consume, use, reduce, reuse, share and recycle as sustainably as we can.

reduce - reuse - recycle - reinvent

Reduce, reuse, recycle is the great ecological and systemic mantra within our culture of mass consumption. This is so important, yet so taken for granted. 'Reinvent' is a new addition to the three R's.

If we took things back to the drawing board and insisted on using the latest technology we could make products using a fraction of the resources and energy required to build, maintain and run them.
Factor Four, the report to the Club of Rome (1997) by Ernst Von Weizacker, Amory B. Lovins and L. Hunter Lovins pointed this out so successfully.
In Factor Four everyday items such as light bulbs, motor cars, washing machines and fridges are redesigned using current technology so as to reduce by at least a factor of four (that's a quarter) the fuel required to build and run such items. A simple example would be electro-magnetic brakes on cars that don't need to rely on friction, therefore no wear and tear.
I believe it should be illegal to make energy that is unsustainably sourced. The production of globally sustainable energy could be achieved using a fraction of the amount of money spent on arms and weaponry worldwide.
When will we as a species stop squabbling and fighting over resources?

What role can we play in this transition?

What is the critical mass needed to make this sort of shift?
All packaging could, by law, or by financial incentive, be reduced to the bare minimum and be recyclable. Manufacturers could also be required to pay for any ecological costs of the products they make.
Instead of pushing costs onto the consumer or more usually the environment and the tax-payer, manufacturers could be required to deal with the systemic chaos created through using ecologically unsound packaging and manufacturing systems.
It's estimated that there are fifteen carrier bags of plastic waste for every single metre of coastline on the planet, just floating in the oceans, that is more than the surface area of the U.K. The consequences of this waste is devastating to oceanic lifeforms and causing plenty of systemic chaos.
Many industries, such as mining, are becoming much more responsible and creative in pre-empting the environmental damage that our activities can create. We need much, much more proactive attention to the environmental consequences of all our human activities, not less.
The bare minimum we can do as practitioners of conscious co-evo-

lution is to reduce all unnecessary consumption, reuse all materials possible, and recycle everything else. Ideally there would be nothing left to go into landfills.
Could we collectively support and push through political process via the power of our wallets, votes and action, thereby generating greater effectiveness and awareness of the four key processes of reduction, re-use, recycling and reinventing?

Could we push for intelligently reinvented products that use state of the art technology?

Could we support technology that minimises the use of energy and resources for the production, maintenance, use and recycling of all the products we use in our lives?

As global citizens we could also be proactive in encouraging recalcitrant leaders of governments, media and industry to pay attention to ecological systemics.
Systemic realisation in conscious co-evolution is the deep kinaesthetic knowledge of our total inter-relationship with all life-form. We are dependent on bees. Remember, all of life is interdependent. Bees in fact would survive better without us, not so easy the other way around, despite the recent creation of a robotic bee in Japan.
Substantial research clearly indicates that our fossil fuel burning activities are disturbing water systems, air systems, planetary thermals, and are putting the lives of cold-blooded invertebrates and oceanic life at stake.
Lets pay attention, now.
Are there any governments that have good clear and proactive environmental records?

Despite the political appearances and green-wash prevalent on this planet, there is no concerted effort to create a real global council that will seek and utilise expert opinion to manage and steward our planet. Decisions continue to be made as if every nation were separate from every other nation, as if the environmental degradation caused by one country doesn't affect us all. Realising inseparability, greater numbers of us (humans) will be paying attention and really work together on these key issues of our time.

My belief is that we need to build a proactive and awakened global culture of stewardship where all tribes, all nations, all peoples work harmoniously to create mutual wellbeing and mutual prosperity.
What actions can and will we take to co-create the awakened culture that will create a habitable planet for our children and our children's children?
Remember the mantra?

Reduce - Reuse - Recycle - Reinvent - and to add to that Share.

energy production

For society to survive we need energy. Whether the energy comes from burning wood, coal, from nuclear fusion or fission, or from the wind and sun we still need energy.

If we look into world history we find that pre-industrial societies all gained their energy from slavery. Every culture built their world on slavery of some kind or another. Slavery is still happening, whether its wage slavery, sexual slavery through human traffic, workers in sweat shops, or mistreated migrant workers building vast castles to commerce in desert landscapes for fossil fuel magnates, yes it is still happening. But let's not point it out, that would be inconvenient, yet another inconvenient truth.

Given we don't want a return to greater levels of slavery.
Given we have to give up our addiction to burning fossil fuels for energy, where are we going to get our energy from?

Nuclear is getting cleaner, fission is getting cleaner and there is the possibility of fusion.
Do we go nuclear?

The post-fission cleaning up process is still highly problematic though. We don't have effective ways to deal with all the waste and it is totally unfair to leave that problem to future generations.
In my view, we should not use technologies that require us to indebt and burden our descendants.

What's your view?

Solar concentrating mirrors, better quality photovoltaics along with some wind power, some wave power, some hydro-power, some geo-thermal, some bio-mass conversion, all this collectively would allow global energy requirements to be met quite easily. With a mosaic of these techniques of generation we could easily provide our global energy needs.

Why aren't we doing it?

Where are the vested interests blocking such development?

Can these blockages be resolved?

What will it take to shift them?

Solar concentrating mirrors have been shown to be able to meet global electricity demands with only a few hundred square miles of desert surface. But then we would need global communication and sharing of this resource, whilst at the moment we behave like squabbling tribes fighting over every square inch of territory and resource. There is no real united nations yet.

Then there is the possibility, again well tested, of growing blue-green algae that will both break down our waste products and purify waste water as well as giving the means for creating fuel. Blue-green algae produce huge amounts of oil, all of it carbon-neutral.

All the methods mentioned above in the mosaic of energy generations strategies work. They are not being effectively implemented because we are waiting for the market to catch up.

Will the human species be in danger of rapid extinction by the time thelethargic market, riddled with vested interests finally catches up?

Along with renewable power sourcing, surely we could also pay attention to energy conservation?

Efficient insulation, sustainable and well-engineered cooling systems, and attention to all new building design as well as old structure conversion to appropriate eco standards could be a priority.

Why is it not a priority?

Why is this not happening rapidly?

What is needed to make it happen more fully?

In what ways are you prepared to reduce your energy consumption? How will we build a culture of appropriately lower energy consumption?

Given the trillions of dollars spent annually on weapons provision and warfare, would this money be more wisely spent on providing sustainable energy production systems.
Or am I missing something?

transport - getting around

We all travel. I try to go by train and public transport as often as possible. My personal vehicle runs on bio-diesel made from recycled vegetable oil, this is relatively okay as its a twenty-five year old vehicle which has worked to cover the carbon footprint of its production. The particulate pollution from diesels, even bio-diesels is a problem though.
We live in a world where almost all transport infrastructures are fossil fuel dependent, a world where almost any sustainable transport choice other than cycling is not available.
How do any of us get around with any real level of carbon sensitivity when global infrastructure is so carbon confined?

What alternatives could be available to us?
Why aren't they?

Could we develop mag-lev vehicular pods that sit on rails during inter-city transits and drop into an individualised mode, running on solar generated electric, when inside an urban environment?

Can we use trains more and power these with sustainably produced electric?

How about more mag-lev trains that have less moving parts?

How about the hybrid airplanes running on bio-fuels that have already been tested in prototype?

Sustainable aviation fuel has been made with the help of blue green algae, why are we not investing large scale in this? Why are airlines not insisting on its development?

How can developers and investors be encouraged to pay attention to exciting new and old possibilities?

How can we be more active in demanding cleaner transportation that is fossil fuel free?

What are the most effective strategies to reduce fossil fuel dependence and encourage transport providers to come up with the goods, fossil-fuel-free transport for all?

Obviously walking and cycling are part of the way forward.
Why does it appear that industry leaders are not paying attention to cutting edge developments that can lead to a more sustainable world?

How can we help them to pay attention and prioritise ecological concerns over profit and returning dividend to their investors. Aren't they and their investors also residents of planet earth?

How can we show how serious we are about this and help governments and industry to understand that it is in their and our interest to be proactive in investing in sustainable development?

How will we encourage city planners to do more than token sustainability programs?

Do residential parking zones really solve the awful problems of congestion, or are they just another fancy urban tax?

How do we resolve urban congestion then?

How can we help to get more energy and money behind making all cities green and make all city transport and inter-city transport completely integrated and sustainable?

China are doing it, building carbon-neutral buildings and cities.
We have the technology. We really do. Yet we appear to lack the incentive, the relevant investment and the concerted political will.
What is our role in encouraging these three key missing elements?

Remember, inordinate sums of money are spent on weapons technology, weapons purchase, the losing battle against drugs and pornography every single year.
Why are these resources not being spent on sustainability instead?

We have the money and the technology, yet where is the investment and the concerted, focused political will to action the generation and provision of sustainable transportation?

Surely it is time?

wellbeing

Intelligent yogic practice at its best is a preventative, rejuvenative and therapeutic medicine that can prevent, heal or help many health and wellbeing related problems.
The body is constantly seeking balance and healing. It consistently seeks balance (homeostasis) within both the capacity and limits of its evolution.
I know through direct experience the relationship between mind, breath, feelings, body and environment.
Wouldn't it be fabulous if this subjective experience was, at last, taken seriously and became objective through the inquiry of empiricism?

We know the power of mind focused through belief. The most tested contemporary medicine is placebo. Researchers have even tested placebos when people know they are placebos and if they are told the placebo worked for other people then it still works. We are working with the power of belief in Engaged Yoga, not the power of placebo.
We really would do well to empirically test the power of belief and sug-

gestion and start using these powers of the mind ideally to prevent and secondly to help heal medical problems.
Most people to harness their powers of belief have to have an overarching meta-narrative, a big story that has all the answers. Traditionally this was religion and belief in authorities. Now, many still need this hence the New Age belief systems that have arisen to offer support to our own healing processes. The big story or big authority allowed us to suspend our rational disbelief and harness the healing powers of belief. Can we suspend the need for meta-narratives and still harness the power of belief. Conscious co-evolution says yes we can.
Yes we can harness and harvest the power of our own belief. Can we do this collectively, let's give it a go.

Asian flow medicines, exemplified by yoga, Ayurveda, martial arts, traditional Chinese medicine, and all their variants, keep their practitioners in high states of optimal wellbeing. I call them flow medicines because they seek to facilitate internal flow as a means to prevent the origination of disease.
If we stay in flow we stay in wellbeing, this is the general principle of these preventative approaches to wellbeing.
Through the study of factors that work best to sustain optimal wellbeing, optimal function and positive psychology we could cultivate a global culture of preventative and rejuvenative medicine.
This is slowly beginning to happen.

Positive psychology is a good example of empirically based practices that facilitate wellbeing. Even here there are many empirically validated practices missing from the repertoire of positive psychology. These missing components include..

- being in nature
- meditation
- mindfulness
- good somatics practice
- all the different facets of exercise
- touch

A culturally approved preventative medicine would save millions of dollars, euros, pounds, yen, yuan, rupees, or whatever currency you

prefer. Prevention is always better than cure. Curative medicine is much more expensive.
Contemporary curative medicine is mostly wonderful and if I had a damaging car crash I would demand the attentions of a contemporary western trained doctor not an Ayurvedic practitioner, despite my fondness for Ayurveda.
What else do we need to pay attention to with medicine and wellbeing?

rethinking everything

Resolute inquiry is the capacity to continuously and deeply inquire in a consistently powerful way into every aspect of…

- Nature
- Meaning
- Purpose
- Randomness
- Teachings
- Experience
- Identity
- Unicity
- Multiplicity
- Life
- Existence

Resolute inquiry explores paradox, and like zen koans (puzzles offered by meditation teachers to students. These puzzles cannot be understood or answered rationally. It is only insight that can resolve the paradox of koan) takes us into realisation and comfort with paradox.

Inquiry of this kind is liberating and evolutionary.
It questions everything and rethinks everything.
There is no point in repeating negative patterns from the past when we see their consequences.
Conscious co-evolution offers us some of the awareness tools to look deep into these patterns and discard what no longer serves us.
Every meditation practice is an inquiry, it's not supposed to be a form of habituation, it's intended to generate clarity, presence-being and

spontaneity in response to this moment and it's arising phenomena.
Every time you practise, every time you sit, vow to awaken. Prepare to awaken in this practice.
Be utterly present in this moment.
Let this moment be one of full presence

Re-cognising we are intimate connection, that we are relational beings, we know we are the interdependent web of life. We are also the unique and individual, conventional experience of permeable and fractal boundary that we can laughingly call 'Me' and 'You'.
Let us use this day wisely, enjoy and deepen in resolute inquiry. Let any arising insight permeate every level and every aspect of our life and bring us all to greater and more conscious co-evolution.

To make the difference that makes the difference we are going to have to rethink everything, re-dream everything and manifest a whole new way of being on this planet that is no longer rooted in the vision of superiority of homo-sapiens over other species, the entitlement of homo-sapiens to this planet or its ecology or possession of it's surface. Such a vision of humans as part of nature, and yet it's stewards, is possible, even though a rather large ask when we are still in times of massive ecological desecration.
Ecologists are telling us that half the species currently existing on this planet (and we've already made so many extinct) will be extinct by the next century, based completely on the assumption that we will make it that far. But either way we have work to do.
We can do it still despite the current reactionary phase of separatist, materialist, supremacist, masculist, ecocidal, consumption oriented and profit driven mania.
We can do it because we will pull together in concerted action that re-dreams, rethinks, recreates and revisions everything in a powerful new way.
Let's do it together.

If what is written in this book agrees with reason, stands up to scrutiny and is conducive to the good and gain of one and all, then I invite you to live by it.

Christopher Gladwell

This book is simply the result of being an inquiring human being in a complex world of paradox and change.

This synergy of exploration, bound with a passion for liberating change, a love of life and real care for our planetary home is an invitation to a wholesome future.

I invite you to share this work and build a movement of humanity that is passionate about realising our human potential, through living the kind of vision embodied in this book.

Let's get really passionate about creating social and ecological change to make this planet inhabitable for our children and our children's children to the nth generation.
This, in my view, is our responsibility.

I teach in the UK and internationally, and I thank you for the opportunity to share my work with you via this book, via my other books and through my retreats.

Find me at...

www.christophergladwell.com